CRIMINAL JUSTICE

IN FLORIDA

THIRD EDITION

ELLEN G. COHN

Florida International University

PEARSON

Prentice
Hall

Upper Saddle River, New Jersey 07458

Executive Editor: Frank Mortimer, Jr.
Assistant Editor: Sara Holle
Production Editor: Barbara Cappuccio
Director of Manufacturing and Production: Bruce Johnson
Managing Editor: Mary Carnis
Manufacturing Buyer: Cathleen Petersen
Creative Director: Cheryl Asherman
Cover Design Coordinator: Miguel Ortiz
Cover Design: Denise Brown
Cover Image: Day Williams/Photo Researchers, Inc.

Pearson Prentice Hall™ is a trademark of Pearson Education, Inc.
Pearson® is a registered trademark of Pearson plc
Prentice Hall® is a registered trademark of Pearson Education, Inc.

Pearson Education LTD.
Pearson Education Singapore, Pte. Ltd
Pearson Education, Canada, Ltd
Pearson Education–Japan
Pearson Education Australia PTY, Limited
Pearson Education North Asia Ltd
Pearson Educaçion de Mexico, S.A. de C.V.
Pearson Education Malaysia, Pte. Ltd

PEARSON
Prentice
Hall

10 9 8 7 6 5 4 3 2 1
ISBN 0-13-114028-0

CONTENTS

PREFACE

This text will provide you with specific information on the Florida criminal justice system and the Florida criminal law. Throughout the book, you will find a number of quotations which have been taken verbatim from various legal documents, such as the Florida Statutes and the Florida Constitution. Any misspellings or other irregularities are reproduced exactly as they appear in the original documents.

I hope that you enjoy this book and find it both interesting and informative. If you have any questions, comments, or suggestions, please feel free to contact me.

Ellen G. Cohn, Ph.D.
cohne@fiu.edu

CHAPTER 1

THE STATE OF FLORIDA

INTRODUCTION

Florida is located in the southeastern region of the United States and is the southernmost state on the mainland. It consists of a low-lying peninsula which borders both the Atlantic Ocean and the Gulf of Mexico, as well as a long strip of land in the northwest which is known as the panhandle. The northern portion of the panhandle borders on Alabama and Georgia. Tallahassee, the capital of Florida, is located in the panhandle region. The state bird is the mockingbird, the state flower is the orange blossom, the state animal is the panther, and the state tree is the Sabal palmetto palm. Florida's nickname is the "Sunshine State."

THE HISTORY OF FLORIDA

The First Spanish Rule of Florida

Florida was originally occupied by a variety of Native American tribes belonging to three main nations: the Apalachee, the Timucua, and the Calusa. These tribes, which numbered approximately 350,000 prior to the arrival of European settlers in the early 16th century, lived in agricultural settlements. These tribes no longer exist in Florida, due both to their lack of resistance to European-born diseases such as smallpox and measles, and to their vulnerability to English slaving raids during the 17th and 18th centuries.

The first Europeans to occupy Florida were the Spanish. The Spanish explorer, Juan Ponce de León, who is generally believed to have been the first European in the region, landed there in April 1513. He claimed the region for Spain and named it Florida. He returned in 1521 with an expedition of approximately 200 settlers and started a colony on Florida's Gulf Coast. Other Spanish explorers who visited Florida during the 16th century included Pánfilo de Narváez and Hernando de Soto, both of whom led expeditions into Florida in search of gold.

In 1562, a group of Huguenots, or French Protestants, started a settlement near the mouth of the Saint Johns River. In 1564, they built Fort Caroline near what is now Jacksonville. The religious nature of the settlement produced objections from Roman Catholic Spain and, in 1565, the Spanish governor of Florida, Pedro Menendez de Avilés, attacked the fort and killed most of the occupants. A Spanish garrison was placed on the site of Fort Caroline; in 1567, a French expedition destroyed it in retaliation for the attack on the fort. In 1565, Menendez also founded St. Augustine, the first permanent European settlement in the United States. By the middle of the 17th century, Spain had built a series of missions running from St. Augustine to what is now Tallahassee.

Starting in the early 17th century, both England and France began to encroach upon the area held by Spain. England established settlements in North and South Carolina and in Georgia. In the early 18th century, the English, along with Native Americans of the Yamasee and Creek nations, began to attack Spanish settlements in northern Florida, destroying the missions and killing or enslaving most of the Apalachee and Timucua tribes. The French established settlements in Mississippi, Louisiana, and Alabama and, in 1719, captured the Spanish settlement at Pensacola; it was returned to Spanish rule in 1722. By 1750, Great Britain controlled much of the Atlantic Coast while France controlled the Gulf Coast west of Pensacola.

British Rule of Florida

The French and Indian War (also known as the Seven Years War) between France and Great Britain lasted from 1754 to 1763. During this period, Spain became allied with France against Great Britain. The first battle of the war took place in 1754 when the French defeated colonial troops, led by then-Major George Washington. In the first years of the war, France had several key military successes against the British and colonial soldiers. However, in 1758, the tide turned and the British began to dominate the war. In 1759, the French were severely damaged by the fall of Quebec and in 1760, British troops captured Montreal. The war ended with the signing of the Treaty of Paris in 1763. As a result of this treaty, Great Britain gained a large amount of land, including Florida. The territory was divided into two separate colonies. East Florida included most of what is now the state of Florida, whereas West Florida consisted of the rest of the state as well as parts of what are now Alabama, Mississippi, and Louisiana.

Great Britain ruled Florida for the next 21 years, and the colony became home to settlers from many parts of Europe. Florida was not involved in the Revolutionary War. Although the thirteen original colonies invited both East and West Florida to join them in declaring independence from Great Britain, Florida remained loyal to the English king and became a refuge for British Loyalists fleeing Georgia and South Carolina. After Spain formed an alliance with the colonists and entered the war, several attacks were made on West Florida. Mobile was captured in 1780, and Pensacola in 1781. In 1783, after the Revolution ended, a second Treaty of Paris formally returned both East and West Florida to Spain.

The Second Spanish Rule of Florida

After the second Treaty of Paris, Spain maintained control of Florida until 1821, making it the only part of southeastern North America that was not part of the new United States. During this period, immigrants from the new United States began to settle in the region. The U.S. government encouraged this settlement as well as the increasing interest in the possibility that Florida might be annexed by the U.S. Spain paid little attention to Florida, aside from maintaining garrisons or forts in the main ports. The Seminole Indians were living in Florida during this period. Georgia residents resented the Seminoles, partly because they desired the land occupied by the tribe and also because they were greatly angered by the willingness of the Seminoles to harbor fugitive slaves escaping south from Georgia.

During the War of 1812, the British obtained permission from Spain to set up a naval base at Pensacola. In 1814, American troops led by General Andrew Jackson attacked and captured Pensacola, giving the U.S. a new foothold in the territory. During the First Seminole War, which ran from 1817 to 1819, border raids by the Seminole resulted in an invasion of Florida by U.S. troops, led by General Jackson. Jackson's actions, which included the capture, court-martial, and execution of two British traders who had incited the Seminole, as well as a second capture of Pensacola, angered both Britain and Spain. However, after a long series of negotiations, Spain ceded Florida to the United States in 1819 in the Adams-Onís Treaty; the U.S. formally took possession of Florida in 1821.

Florida as a United States Territory

Andrew Jackson served as the temporary military governor of Florida for several months, until Congress organized the region as a territory and appointed the first territorial governor, William P. DuVal in 1822. In 1824, Tallahassee was named the territorial capital.

A growing number of settlers began to move into the territory, setting up traditional Southern plantations and growing corn, tobacco and cotton. Because much of the best farmland in the region was occupied by the Seminole, settlers had difficulties obtaining sufficient land upon which to settle. As a result, the treat of Paynes Landing was forced upon the Seminole in 1832, requiring them to move west of the Mississippi within three years. However, opposition to this treaty, led by Seminole war leader Osceola, eventually led to the Second Seminole War (1835-1842). The Seminole surrendered in 1842, and the majority of the tribe was moved to what is now Oklahoma, although some remained in the Everglades. A Third Seminole War broke out in 1855. After it ended in 1858, approximately half of the Seminole in the Everglades were also moved west. The remainder, only a few hundred, stayed in Florida and did not sign a formal peace treaty with the United States until 1935.

Florida During the 19th Century

The first Florida state constitution was ratified in 1839, and on March 3, 1845 Florida became the 27th state in the Union, entering the United States as a slave state. The eight-year delay was caused by Congress' desire to maintain a balance between slave and free states (Iowa was admitted as a free state in 1846). The first state governor was William D. Moseley. During the next 15 years, the new state's population doubled, although most people settled in the northern regions of the state. Florida was an agricultural state and the primary crop was cotton which was grown by slaves on plantations. In addition, residents raised cattle and produced lumber, leather, salt, and turpentine.

Prior to the Civil War, Florida representatives to Congress fought to retain slavery in the United States. Florida officially seceded from the Union on January 10, 1861, under pressure from the state's pro-slavery Democratic party, and later joined the Confederate States of America. Although Union troops captured a number of coastal towns (including Jacksonville, Pensacola, and St. Augustine) early in the Civil War, Tallahassee remained the only Confederate capital east of the Mississippi River which was not occupied by Union troops during the Civil War. The only major battle of the War to be fought in Florida occurred at Olustee on February 20, 1864. The Confederates defeated the Union troops in this battle, allowing the Confederacy to maintain control of the interior of the state.

When the Civil War ended in 1865, President Johnson appointed a Provisional Governor, William Marvin, to reorganize the Florida state government and draw up a new constitution which formally abolished slavery. However, the new government, which was still dominated by former Confederates who opposed the abolition of slavery, proceeded to enact the "Black Codes" which greatly restricted the rights of newly-freed slaves. Under the Republican's Radical Reconstruction plan, Florida was placed under military rule until the state adopted a constitution acceptable to Congress. On June 25, 1868, after Florida ratified a new constitution and accepted the Fourteenth Amendment to the Constitution, it was readmitted to the Union. However, through the use of violence, intimidation, and other terrorist activities against blacks, the Democrats, who were committed to white supremacy, returned to power in 1876. As a way of keeping blacks in an inferior position, their voting rights were restricted through a variety of techniques, including the passage of a Florida poll tax in the late 1880s. Legislation providing for racial segregation in Florida was passed in the late 19th century.

After the Civil War, the falling price of cotton severely hurt Florida farmers, contributing to the development of farmers' alliances, or cooperatives. Their Ocala Platform, adopted in 1890, led to the creation of a new political party, the People's Party. However, although the party was on the ballot in 1892, the inability of many black farmers (who strongly supported the People's Party) to vote in the election, allowed the Democratic Party to maintain its control over Florida into the next century.

The southern portion of Florida was more fully developed after the 1880s, due to the interest of several real estate developers who promoted Florida as a resort. During World War I, when international travel by Americans was significantly restricted, Florida became an increasingly more popular resort destination. In addition, in response to several severe winters, Florida citrus growers began to move further southward to reduce the risk of frost damage to their crops. The development of railroads built by Henry Flagler and Henry Plant also helped to develop the southern portion of the state. In 1860, the swampland near Ft. Lauderdale was drained, opening up additional land for both resorts and farming.

Florida During the 20th Century

After World War I, Florida became even more popular as both a tourist destination and a permanent residence, causing an economic boom and a significant increase in the state's population. Seven new counties were formed in 1921 alone. However, in 1926, the state experienced a severe depression. The real estate market collapsed, land values dropped significantly, and many banks failed. Two extremely destructive hurricanes, which hit the Atlantic coast of Florida in 1926 and 1928, also contributed to the state's economic collapse. Despite this, Florida's tourist industry showed continued growth and, by 1929, the economy was beginning to recover. Although the state experienced a drop in tourism during the Great Depression, federal and state aid programs assisted in the continued improvement of Florida's economy through the development of paper mills, forest conservation programs, cooperative farm groups, and cooperative markets.

Florida's location made the state a key defense link during World War II. A number of land, sea, and air bases were established, and several million American servicemen and servicewomen were trained in Florida.

After World War II, the construction of the Air Force Missile Test Center at Cape Canaveral established Florida as a national center for American space exploration. The first U.S. earth satellite (1958), the first manned U.S. space flight (1961), and the first manned space flight to the moon (1969) were all launched from Cape Canaveral. In addition, Florida's tourist industry continued to increase. The development of attractions such as Walt Disney World near Orlando, as well as the state's many beaches, drew millions of visitors, many of whom settled permanently in Florida. The state also developed industries in a variety of areas, including electronics, paper and paper products, and chemicals.

After the Castro-led revolution overthrew the Batista government in 1959, a Communist government was set up in Cuba. As a result, approximately 11,000 Cubans, many of whom who had opposed the Communist regime, fled the country and settled in south Florida, mostly in Miami and Hialeah. A second wave of Cuban immigration occurred in 1961, when the immigration ban was briefly lifted. During the next forty years, immigrants from many other Latin American countries, such as El Salvador, Colombia, and Venezuela also settled in Miami-Dade County, resulting in the rise of Miami as an important center for international banking and trade. Since 1980, over 100,000 Cuban and Haitian refugees have settled in Florida.

The 1980s and 1990s brought a variety of concerns for the state. Environmental pollution is a major issue. Florida currently has over 50 hazardous waste sites which are on the EPA's national priority list. The Everglades waterways sustained significant damage due to chemical pollution, and significant efforts at both the state and federal level are focusing on reversing the damage. Other concerns included significant crime problems, which were aggravated by the increasing amounts of marijuana and cocaine being smuggled into the state from Colombia, Bolivia, and Peru. Several major natural disasters in the 1990s resulted in significant damage and deaths. Hurricane Andrew, which hit southern Florida in 1992, is considered to be the most expensive natural disaster in the history of the United States. Andrew was followed three years later by Hurricanes Erin and Opal, and, in 1998, by a series of tornadoes which swept across central Florida.

The 2000 presidential election brought the attention of the world to Florida because the state's 25 electoral college votes were the deciding factor in determining the outcome of the election. Although Republican candidate George W. Bush was declared the eventual winner, the various technical problems uncovered in the state's voting process created a considerable amount of concern and frustration, and led many to claim that the entire election process had been compromised. The 2001 Florida Election Reform Act was designed to correct many of the voting problems for future elections.

FLORIDA TODAY

Florida is the 23rd largest state in the country, with a total land area of 53,927 square miles, as well as 4,683 square miles of inland water and 1,308 square miles of costal water over which the state has jurisdiction. The peninsula portion of the state has an average width of approximately 125 miles. At the southern tip of the peninsula is a chain of small islands known as the Florida Keys. The average elevation of the state is 100 feet above sea level; the highest point, located in the panhandle is 345 feet above sea level. Florida has more miles of coastline (1,350 miles) than any other state except Alaska.

Florida's largest single source of income is tourism. The most popular tourist attractions include the various theme parks and other attractions in and near Orlando, as well as the resorts and beaches along the state's coastline, such as Miami, Miami Beach, Fort Lauderdale, St. Petersburg, and Daytona Beach. As a result, the service industry is extremely important in Florida, with much of the industry being devoted to the needs of tourists. Other important sources of economic activity include farming (particularly citrus fruits) and manufacturing (particularly electronics, printing and publishing, and transportation equipment).

Currently, Florida is the fourth most populous state in the country (after California, Texas, and New York). The 2000 census reported a total population of 15,982,378, an increase of 23.5 percent over the 1990 figure, making Florida one of the fastest-growing states in the country. The most populous city is Jacksonville, with an estimated population of 735,617 in 2000. Other cities with a population of over 100,000 include Miami, Tampa, St. Petersburg, Hialeah, Orlando, Ft. Lauderdale, Tallahassee, Hollywood, and Pembroke Pines. Miami-Dade county is the largest county by population, with 2,253,362 inhabitants in 2000. The largest county by area is Palm Beach County, with 2,034 square miles. The oldest continually-inhabited city in the United States is St. Augustine. Population estimates represent only permanent residents, excluding people such as tourists and seasonal residents (commonly known as "snowbirds").[1]

According to the 2000 census, people over the age of 65 make up approximately 17.6 percent of the population of Florida (significantly higher than the national average of 12.4 percent). This disparity is due primarily to the many senior citizens from around the country and from Canada who move to the state after retiring. The census shows that approximately 78 percent of the state's population are white and 14.6 percent are black; the rest of the population includes Asians, Pacific Islanders, and Native Americans. Almost 17 percent of the population are reported as being of Hispanic origin, although they may be of any race.[2] Most of the population lives in urban areas. Much of the southern portion of the state, including a large part of the Everglades as well as many of the islands along the Gulf Coast, is virtually uninhabited. There are several Native American reservations in Florida; one is located north and east of Lake Okeechobee, while another is northwest of the Everglades, in Big Cypress Swamp.

Florida has a total of 67 counties. The state elects two United States Senators and 23 members of the House of Representatives, for a total of 25 electoral votes. The current state constitution was adopted in 1968.

NOTES

1.   U.S. Census Bureau (http://www.census.gov)
2.   *Ibid.*

CHAPTER 2

INTRODUCTION TO FLORIDA CRIMINAL LAW

THE STRUCTURE OF THE GOVERNMENT

Florida criminal law is found in the state constitution and in the Florida Statutes. Both have been frequently modified, amended, and altered over the past 150 years.

The first **Florida State Constitution**[1] was ratified in 1839, six years before Florida became a state. The current (sixth) constitution was adopted in 1968. The Florida State Constitution is the primary law of the state, although it is of course subordinate to the United States Constitution. No criminal law or constitutional amendment enacted in Florida may conflict with or violate any individual rights which are guaranteed by the U.S. Constitution, the Bill of Rights, any other Constitutional Amendments, or any federal laws. If any part of the Florida State Constitution or legal code is found to be in conflict with the U.S. Constitution or federal statutes, the Florida enactment is unconstitutional and must be changed.

There are four different ways in which the Florida State Constitution may be amended or revised. These are described in Article XI of the Florida State Constitution. First, a new amendment or revision may be proposed by a joint resolution that is agreed to by three-fifths of the membership of each house of the **Florida State Legislature**. Second, the constitution may be amended by a 37-member **revision commission** appointed by the legislature. Third, it may be amended through the **initiative** process, which involves Florida voters presenting a petition which has been signed by a specified number of voters. Finally, the people have the right to call a **constitutional convention** for the purpose of considering a revision of the entire state constitution. This process also requires a petition signed by a specified number of voters; the question of whether a constitutional convention should be held is then presented to the voters and if a majority of voters agree, representatives are elected and the constitutional convention is convened.

Regardless of which method is used, any proposed amendments or revisions must be approved by the voters of the state. If the proposed amendment is passed at a general election, it becomes effective on the first Tuesday after the first Monday in January following the election, unless a different date is specified in the amendment or revision.

Like most states, Florida has three branches of government: executive, legislative, and judicial. This is specified in Article II, Section 3 of the Florida Constitution.

The Executive Branch

Article IV of the Florida Constitution discusses Florida's **executive branch**, which consists of a governor, a lieutenant governor, and a cabinet. The cabinet includes an attorney general, a chief financial officer, and a commissioner of agriculture.

The governor and lieutenant governor are elected to four-year terms and may not serve more than two consecutive terms. However, after the passage of the next term, they is eligible to serve again. They are elected jointly, so that voters cast a single vote for both candidates. Members of the cabinet are also elected to four-year terms but may serve any number of consecutive terms. To be elected to the office of governor or lieutenant-governor of Florida, or to the state cabinet, candidates must, at the time of election, be an elector at least 30 years-of-age and have been resident in the state for the preceding seven years. Candidates for attorney general also must have been a member of the Florida Bar for at least five years preceding election to office. The term of office for the governor, lieutenant governor, and all cabinet members begins on the first Tuesday after the first Monday in January of the year following election to office.

The executive branch also includes a variety of executive departments and agencies that are responsible for state programs. They are supervised by the governor, lieutenant governor, cabinet, or some officer appointed by the governor for that purpose.

The governor has the power to veto legislation that has been proposed by the state legislature. However, a two-thirds vote in both houses of the legislature may override the governor's veto.

On January 5, 1999, John Ellis "Jeb" Bush, the younger brother of President George W. Bush, became the 43rd governor of Florida. Governor Bush, who is a Republican, was re-elected in November 2002. He is the first Republican in Florida ever to be re-elected to a second term as governor. His present term expires in January 2007, and he is not eligible to run in the November 2006 gubernatorial election.

The Legislative Branch

The **state legislature** is discussed in Article III of the Florida Constitution and is the lawmaking branch of the state government. The Florida legislature is made up of two houses: a 40-member Senate and a 120-member House of Representatives. Because the two houses have equal shares in the power of lawmaking, there are no rights or powers in the legislative process that are not shared by both houses. Either house has the right to originate any type of legislation. As well as its primary lawmaking duties, the legislature does have several semi-judicial functions. For example, the House has the exclusive right to impeach officers, whereas the Senate alone has the power to try such accused officers.

Each member of the legislature represents one senatorial or representative district. Senators are elected to four-year terms, with half the members elected every two years to allow for staggered terms. Members of the House of Representatives are elected to two-year terms. There is no limit to the number of times members of the legislature may be re-elected, but no member may serve more than eight consecutive years. To serve as a member of the Florida state legislature, candidates must be at least twenty-one years-of-age, a resident of the district from which s/he is elected, and have been a Florida state resident for at least two years prior to the election. Members take office immediately upon election. Each house selects its own officers from among its membership. The presiding officer of the Senate is known as the President of the Senate; the Senate may also designate a Secretary. The presiding officer of the House of Representatives is known as the Speaker of the House of Representatives. The House also selects a Clerk.

Meetings of the state legislature are held annually in Tallahassee. **Regular Sessions**, which may run for no more than sixty consecutive days, are usually convened on the first Tuesday after the first Monday in March. There are also seven additional types of legislative sessions which may be convened:

- An **Organization Session** is required by the constitution to be convened on the fourteenth day following a state-wide general election. The purpose of this special session is to organize the legislature and select officers. While there is no time limit on an organization session, it usually lasts approximately two hours.

- A **Special Session** of the legislature, which may run no longer than twenty consecutive days, may be convened by the governor or by a three-fifths vote of each house. The length of legislative sessions may be extended only by a three-fifths majority vote in both houses.

- An **Apportionment Session**, which may run a maximum of thirty consecutive days, is convened by the governor if he believes the legislature has failed to properly reapportion the representation in the Senate and House of Representatives.

- A **Self-Starter Session** occurs when the legislature convenes itself for a period of not more than thirty days. This type of session can only be convened by a three-fifths vote of all members of the legislature. In the history of the Florida Legislature, there have been three unsuccessful attempts to call the legislature into a Self-Starter Session; the most recent was in 1972.

- A special session that only involves the Senate is the **Suspension Session of Senate**, which may be called for the purpose of considering the suspension of the governor or a state or county officer.

- The President of the Senate and the Speaker of the House of Representatives may convene the legislature in special session by jointly calling a **Session Called by Presiding Officers**.

- Finally, the legislature may extend the length of any regular or special session through an **Extended Session**, which requires a three-fifths vote of the membership of both houses. The purpose of an extended session is to complete action on legislation that has already been introduced.

The Judicial Branch

The judicial branch of the government, which is discussed in Article V of the Florida Constitution, contains the various Florida courts. These include a state supreme court, district courts of appeal, circuit courts, and county courts. The highest court in the state is the **Florida Supreme Court**, which is made up of seven justices. The justices select one member from amongst themselves to serve as chief justice. Supreme Court justices are appointed by the governor from recommendations made by a state judicial nominating commission and serve six-year terms; when a justice's term expires, his or her name is brought forth at the next general election for a merit retention vote. In addition, each of the five appellate districts in the state has a **District Court of Appeal**, which is composed of at least three judges. District courts hear appeals from county and circuit courts. Like Supreme Court justices, district court judges also serve six-year terms.

Each of the 20 judicial circuits is served by a **Circuit Court** which has original jurisdiction over all cases not heard by the county courts, including criminal felonies, juvenile cases, and civil cases involving at least $2,500. The circuit court also has appellate jurisdiction in some circumstances. Circuit court judges are elected to six-year terms.

Each of the 67 counties in Florida also has a **County Court**, which has original jurisdiction over all misdemeanor cases, all violations of county and municipal ordinances, and certain civil cases, including all landlord-tenant disputes. County court judges serve four-year terms. The Florida court system is discussed in more detail in Chapter 5.

Passing a Law in Florida

In Florida, a bill may be introduced in either the House or the Senate and, after it has been passed by one of the two legislative houses, it may still be amended in the other. A bill must be sponsored by a legislator (either a senator or representative), and will be referred to the relevant committee for study and review. The committee may amend the bill, fail the bill, or pass the bill. If the bill is passed, it may move on to additional committees or be presented to the full legislative house for a vote.

If the bill passes in one house, it moves on to the other and goes through the same review process. If it is amended, it will return to the first house for a new vote. It is possible for a bill to move back and forth between the two legislative houses many times before agreement as to the final wording is obtained.

For a bill to be passed, it must receive a majority vote in each of the two houses. After both houses agree on the wording of the bill, it goes to the governor for approval. The governor has seven days to veto the bill, which is now known officially as an "act." If the governor approves and signs the act, or if he fails to veto it within seven days, the act becomes law. The legislature may, by a two-thirds vote of each house, enact a bill into law over the governor's veto. After a bill becomes law, it takes effect sixty days after the adjournment of the legislative session. The process of passing a law is discussed in the Florida Constitution in Article III.

Local Government in Florida

Local governmental services in Florida are provided by a county, a municipality, or a special district. Currently there are 67 counties in Florida, approximately 400 municipalities, and approximately 1,000 special districts.

Most of the counties in Florida are governed by a board of five elected county commissioners who are responsible for all county-level government. These commissioners must reside within districts but are elected at large. In addition, county residents may elect a number of other officials, including a sheriff, tax assessor, tax collector, surveyor, circuit court clerk, and superintendent of public instruction.

At the city level, most cities use the council and city manager form of municipal government. However, Orlando, Tampa, and Jacksonville have the mayor-council form. Some cities have municipal governments that have been at least partly consolidated with the county government. There have also been some attempts at completely integrating a county and one or more municipalities. Only one of these attempts, the consolidation of Jacksonville and Duval County, has been truly successful.

THE FLORIDA STATE CRIMINAL LAW

There are several sources of criminal law in Florida. These include:

- federal and state constitutions
- statutory criminal law
- common law
- case law

Together, the Florida State Constitution and the U.S. Constitution provide the basic framework for criminal law, first by focusing on individual rights and on the limitations placed on government power and second, by requiring the establishment of a judicial system. However, neither the federal nor the state constitution significantly emphasizes the creation or definition of crimes.

The primary source of **statutory criminal law** in Florida is the Florida Criminal Code, which is codified in Title XLVI of the Florida Statutes (FS), entitled *Crimes*. The current Florida Criminal Code was enacted in 1974 and applies to any crimes committed on or after October 1, 1975. In addition, other statutes also contain laws which relate to crime and punishment. For example, Title XLVII of the Florida Statutes, which is entitled *Criminal Procedure and Corrections*, contains laws relating to procedures such as arrests, trials, sentencing, and corrections. Many of the civil law sections also include statutes dealing with crimes and punishments. However, FS §11.2427 states that,

> If any section in the civil part of the Florida Statutes, creating a crime or prescribing a punishment, conflicts with any section in the part relating to crimes, the latter shall prevail.

Therefore, the criminal code has priority over any other part of the Florida Statutes when dealing with issues relating to crimes and punishments.

The Florida Criminal Code was originally based on the English **common law**, which became the law of the original thirteen colonies and then evolved into the law of the individual states as they entered the union. FS §775.01 states that:

> The common law of England in relation to crimes, except so far as the same relates to the modes and degrees of punishment, shall be of full force in this state where there is no existing provision by statute on the subject.

Because of this, state courts may use the common law to analyze and interpret the state's criminal code. If a specific crime is not defined in the statutes, the common law definition would be applicable. However, if there is any statute that supercedes the common law, that statute becomes the controlling law for that issue.

The first chapter of the Florida Criminal Code outlines the general purposes of the code and its provisions:

(1) To proscribe conduct that improperly causes or threatens substantial harm to individual or public interest.
(2) To give fair warning to the people of the state in understandable language of the nature of the conduct proscribed and of the sentences authorized upon conviction.
(3) To define clearly the material elements constituting an offense and the accompanying state of mind or criminal intent required for that offense.
(4) To differentiate on reasonable grounds between serious and minor offenses and to establish appropriate disposition for each.

(5) To safeguard conduct that is without fault or legitimate state interest from being condemned as criminal.

(6) To ensure the public safety by deterring the commission of offenses and providing for the opportunity for rehabilitation of those convicted and for their confinement when required in the interests of public protection.[2]

Case law consists of appellate court decisions or opinions which interpret the meaning of the law. Effectively, case law is made by judges when they hand down decisions in court. Because of the principle of *stare decisis*, or precedent, a decision made by a judge in one court will be followed by later judges in the state until the same court reverses its decision or until the decision is overturned by a higher court.

The Florida Criminal Code contains two types of statutory criminal law: substantive and procedural. **Substantive criminal laws** are those laws that define specific crimes and set forth the required punishments associated with each criminal act. The section of the Florida Statutes that defines murder (criminal homicide), is an example of substantive criminal law.[3] **Procedural laws**, on the other hand, focus on the methods that are used to enforce the substantive criminal law. In other words, procedural laws outline the rules that the state must follow when dealing with crimes and criminals. These include the procedures that must be used to investigate crimes, arrest suspects, and carry out formal prosecution. The protection against double jeopardy, which is discussed in FS §910.11, is an example of procedural law.

THE DEFINITION AND CLASSIFICATION OF CRIME

In Florida, a **crime** is defined in FS §775.08(4) simply as "a felony or misdemeanor." **Felonies** are the most serious offenses in Florida. FS §775.08(1) defines a felony as:

> ...any criminal offense that is punishable under the laws of this state, or that would be punishable if committed in this state, by death or imprisonment in a state penitentiary. "State penitentiary" shall include state correctional facilities. A person shall be imprisoned in the state penitentiary for each sentence which, except an extended term, exceeds 1 year.

Felonies are classified into five categories, which are used in the determination of the sentence.[4]

- A **capital felony** is the most serious category and is punishable either by death or life imprisonment without parole. First degree murder is an example of a capital felony.

- A **life felony** committed before October 1, 1983 is punishable by life imprisonment or a term of at least 30 years. A life felony committed on or after October 1, 1983 but before July 1, 1995 is punishable by life imprisonment or a term of at least 40 years. A life felony committed on or after July 1, 1995 is punishable by life imprisonment or by imprisonment for a term of years not exceeding life. Clearly, the perceived seriousness of this category of felony has been increasing during the past two decades. There are only a small number of life felonies in the Florida Criminal Code. Examples of life felonies are treason and the commission of sexual battery on a victim who is at least 12 years of age using actual physical force or the threat of deadly force.

- A **felony of the first degree** is punishable by imprisonment for no more than 30 years, unless the statute specifically provides otherwise. Examples of first degree felonies include committing a robbery or carjacking while carrying a deadly weapon, sexual battery by multiple offenders ("gang rape"), and first degree arson.

- A **felony of the second degree** is punishable by imprisonment for no more than 15 years. Examples of second degree felonies include manslaughter, vehicular homicide, unarmed robbery, and second degree arson.

- A **felony of the third degree** is punishable by imprisonment for no more than five years. Examples of third degree felonies include aggravated assault, felony battery, misprison of treason, and arson committed to defraud the insurer.

For a felony to be considered either a capital or a life felony, it must be specified as such in the statutes. Most other felonies are classified by degree in the statutes. If a crime is defined by statute as a felony, but the statute does not specify the degree of the felony, it is considered to be a third degree felony.[5]

A **misdemeanor** is defined in FS §775.08(2) as:

...any criminal offense that is punishable under the laws of this state, or that would be punishable if committed in this state, by a term of imprisonment in a county correctional facility, except an extended term, not in excess of 1 year...

Like felonies, misdemeanors are also classified by degree. According to FS §775.081(2), a misdemeanor may either be first degree or second degree. If a statute defining a crime as a misdemeanor does not specify the degree, it is considered to be a second degree misdemeanor. FS §775.082(4) outlines the penalties associated with misdemeanors:

- A **misdemeanor of the first degree** is punishable by a definite term of imprisonment of up to one year. Simple battery is one example of a first degree misdemeanor.

16

- **A misdemeanor of the second degree** is punishable by a definite term of imprisonment of up to 60 days. An example of a second degree misdemeanor is simple assault.

Florida also recognizes behaviors which are known as **noncriminal violations**. Although these violations are called "noncriminal" and are not legally crimes, they are considered to be offenses, and individuals who are found guilty of these behaviors will receive a sentence from the court. FS §775.08(3) defines a noncriminal violation as:

> ...any offense that is punishable under the laws of this state, or that would be punishable if committed in this state, by no other penalty than a fine, forfeiture, or other civil penalty. A noncriminal violation does not constitute a crime, and conviction for a noncriminal violation shall not give rise to any legal disability based on a criminal offense. The term "noncriminal violation" shall not mean any conviction for any violation of any municipal or county ordinance..

According to FS §775.082(5), individuals convicted of a noncriminal violation may not be sentenced to a term of imprisonment or to any other punishment that is more severe than a fine, forfeiture, or civil penalty. Examples of noncriminal violations include possession of tobacco products by a person under 18 years of age, various parking violations, and various traffic violations.

Offenders convicted of felonies and misdemeanor offenses may be sentenced to pay a fine, as well as to a term of imprisonment. FS §775.083 outlines the fines for each designated classification of crime, as well as the fines acceptable for offenders committing noncriminal violations. Sentencing and the various types of punishments used in Florida are discussed in more detail in Chapter 6.

DEFENSES TO A CRIMINAL CHARGE

There are a wide variety of defenses to a criminal charge. Many are specifically mentioned in the Florida Statutes or the Florida Rules of Criminal Procedure (Fla. R. Crim. P.)[6]

Alibi

An individual who uses the defense of an **alibi** essentially is claiming that s/he was at another place when the crime was committed and thus could not have committed the crime. For an alibi defense to be effective, it must cover the entire time period when the defendant's presence was necessary to commit the crime. Fla. R. Crim. P. 3.200, entitled *Notice of Alibi*, discusses the procedures that a defendant must follow if s/he plans to offer evidence of an alibi in his or her defense. The defendant, upon receiving a written demand from the prosecutor, is required to provide notice to the prosecution of the intent to claim an alibi as a defense. This notice must be provided at least ten days before the trial. A mutual exchange of witness lists is also required, so that both the prosecution and defense must disclose alibi witnesses prior to the trial. Florida adopted this rule in

1968, modeling it after the Ohio, New York, and New Jersey statutes, and became the fourteenth state in the U.S. to adopt a notice of alibi statute or rule.

Justifications

A defendant who uses a **justification** defense admits to the commission of the criminal act but also claims that it was necessary to commit the act in order to avoid some greater evil or harm. Probably the most well-known justification defense is that of **self-defense**, in which the defendant claims that the use of force against the victim was justifiable because it was the only way the defendant could ensure his or her own safety. The issue of **justifiable use of force** is discussed primarily in Chapter 776 of the Florida Statutes. FS §776.012 discusses the use of force in defense of a person, stating that:

> A person is justified in the use of force, except deadly force, against another when and to the extent that the person reasonably believes that such conduct is necessary to defend himself or herself or another against such other's imminent use of unlawful force. However, the person is justified in the use of deadly force only if he or she reasonably believes that such force is necessary to prevent imminent death or great bodily harm to himself or herself or another or to prevent the imminent commission of a forcible felony.

It is clear from this statute that the amount of force used must be proportionate to the amount of force or threat that the defendant is experiencing. An individual is not justified in using force to resist arrest by a law enforcement officer, unless the officer is using excessive force to make the arrest; in that situation, a person may be justified in the use of reasonable force in self-defense.

This statute also states that deadly force may only be used if the defendant believes that s/he or another person is in immediate danger of death or great bodily harm, or to prevent the other party from committing a forcible felony (which could result in death or great bodily harm to someone). Again, the key issue is self-defense or defense of another. **Deadly force** is defined in FS §776.06(1) as:

> The term "deadly force" means force that is likely to cause death or great bodily harm and includes, but is not limited to:
> (a) The firing of a firearm in the direction of the person to be arrested, even though no intent exists to kill or inflict great bodily harm; and
> (b) The firing of a firearm at a vehicle in which the person to be arrested is riding.

The statute also states that deadly force does not include the firing of a firearm loaded with less-lethal ammunition by a law enforcement or correctional officer in the course of his or her duties.[7]

FS 782.02 specifically discusses the justifiable use of deadly force, stating that:

> The use of deadly force is justifiable when a person is resisting any attempt to murder such person or to commit any felony upon him or her or upon or in any dwelling house in which such person shall be.

FS 776.041 outlines when the defense of justifiable use of force may not be used:

> The justification described ... is not available to a person who:
> (1) Is attempting to commit, committing, or escaping after the commission of, a forcible felony; or
> (2) Initially provokes the use of force against himself or herself, unless:
>   (a) Such force is so great that the person reasonably believes that he or she is in imminent danger of death or great bodily harm and that he or she has exhausted every reasonable means to escape such danger other than the use of force which is likely to cause death or great bodily harm to the assailant; or
>   (b) In good faith, the person withdraws from physical contact with the assailant and indicates clearly to the assailant that he or she desires to withdraw and terminate the use of force, but the assailant continues or resumes the use of force.

The issues of **defense of others** and **defense of home and property** are also covered in Chapter 776 of the Florida Statutes. FS 776.031 states that:

> A person is justified in the use of force, except deadly force, against another when and to the extent that the person reasonably believes that such conduct is necessary to prevent or terminate such other's trespass on, or other tortious or criminal interference with, either real property other than a dwelling or personal property, lawfully in his or her possession or in the possession of another who is a member of his or her immediate family or household or of a person whose property he or she has a legal duty to protect. However, the person is justified in the use of deadly force only if he or she reasonably believes that such force is necessary to prevent the imminent commission of a forcible felony.

This statute, combined with FS 776.012, makes it clear that using force in the defense of a third person is an acceptable justification. It also allows the use of force to protect certain specified types of property. Also notice that FS 782.02, which specified when the use of deadly force was justifiable, did state that an individual may use deadly force to resist an attempt to commit a felony upon a dwelling place in which that individual is present. Because the statute limits this to a dwelling place, one may not use deadly force under this statute to protect real property that is not a dwelling place.

Another justification defense is that of **consent**. This defense claims that the injured person voluntarily consented to the actions that caused the injury. It is most commonly used in sex-related offenses, such as sexual battery. FS 794.011(1)(a) defines consent in the crime of sexual battery as:

> "Consent" means intelligent, knowing, and voluntary consent and does not include coerced submission. "Consent" shall not be deemed or construed to mean the failure by the alleged victim to offer physical resistance to the offender.

Consent that is obtained by some form of coercion, such as through the use or threat of force or violence against the victim or another person, does not constitute a defense of consent. Consent often becomes an important issue in the crime of statutory rape, because the victim is below the age of legal consent and is unable to voluntarily agree to participate in sexual activities. Ignorance of the victim's age is not a legal defense in any sexual battery crime involving a victim below a certain specified age.[8]

Excuses

A defendant using an **excuse** defense is claiming that at the time of the criminal act some circumstance or personal condition creates a situation under which s/he should not be held criminally accountable. Probably the most well-known (and controversial) defense in this category is that of **insanity**. Although the term insanity is no longer used by mental health professionals, it is a legal term referring to a defense that is based on the defendant's claim that s/he was mentally ill or mentally incapacitated at the time of the offense.

According to the *Florida Criminal Jury Instructions*[9], the following conditions are required for a defendant to be considered insane:

- The defendant had a mental disease, defect, or infirmity.

- Because of this mental condition, the defendant did not know what he/she was doing or what the consequences would be, or the defendant did not know that what he/she was doing was wrong.

Florida uses the **M'Naughen Test** for insanity, which requires the defendant to show that he or she was "precluded by mental disease from distinguishing between right and wrong at the time of the act."[10] The state does not recognize a defense of diminished capacity, unless it is sufficient to meet the criteria of M'Naughen, nor does it recognize the irresistible impulse test that is used in some other states.

As with an alibi defense, defendants who plan to set forth a defense of insanity must provide advance notice to the prosecution. Fla. R. Crim. P. 3.216 mandates pre-trial notification of intent to assert defense of insanity of no less than 15 days after arraignment or after filing a written plea of not guilty. However, unlike in the case of an alibi, the prosecution is not required to request or demand this notification; the requirement is totally on the defendant to provide the notice.

If a defendant is acquitted of criminal charges using the insanity defense, s/he will be found **not guilty by reason of insanity**, under Fla. R. Crim. P. 3.217. However, even though the defendant has been acquitted of the charges due to insanity, this does not necessarily mean that s/he will be released from custody. According to FS §916.15(1):

> A defendant acquitted of criminal charges because of a finding of not guilty by reason of insanity may be involuntarily committed pursuant to such finding if the defendant is mentally ill and, because of the illness, is manifestly dangerous to himself or herself or others.

Another defense that falls into the category of excuses is that of **involuntary intoxication**. FS §775.051 states that:

> Voluntary intoxication resulting from the consumption, injection, or other use of alcohol or other controlled substance ... is not a defense to any offense proscribed by law. Evidence of a defendant's voluntary intoxication is not admissible to show that the defendant lacked the specific intent to commit an offense and is not admissible to show that the defendant was insane at the time of the offense, except when the consumption, injection, or use of a controlled substance ... was pursuant to a lawful prescription issued to the defendant by a practitioner...

This statute deals with voluntary intoxication. The statutes do not specifically address the issue of involuntary intoxication as a defense. However, involuntary intoxication does come up when discussing other topics, such as consent. For example, FS §794.011(4)(d), which defines first degree sexual battery, lists as one of the categories of the crime,

> When the offender, without the prior knowledge or consent of the victim, administers or has knowledge of someone else administering to the victim any narcotic, anesthetic, or other intoxicating substance which mentally or physically incapacitates the victim.

Procedural Defenses

A **procedural defense** claims that some form of official procedure was not followed or that procedural law was not properly followed during the investigation or the prosecution of the crime. One procedural defense is the **denial of a speedy trial**. FS §918.015(1) states that, "In all criminal prosecutions the state and the defendant shall each have the right to a speedy trial." This right is also guaranteed in Article I, Section 16 of the Florida Constitution and discussed in the Florida Rules of Criminal Procedure. According to Fla. R. Crim. P. 3.191, the time limit for a trial to be "speedy" varies, depending on whether or not the defendant has demanded a trial, as well as on the seriousness of the crime (misdemeanor or felony) but generally ranges from 60 to 175 days. This time limit may be extended under certain circumstances. Obviously, if the defendant requested an extension, s/he may not later claim that his or her right to a speedy trial was denied. However, if the time limit has not been extended by the defendant's request and if there are no exceptional circumstances which caused a delay (and which are specified in the rule), Fla. R. Crim. P. 3.191(p) states that:

(2) At any time after the expiration of the prescribed time period, the defendant may file a separate pleading entitled "Notice of Expiration of Speedy Trial Time," and serve a copy on the prosecuting authority.

(3) No later than 5 days from the date of the filing of a notice of expiration of speedy trial time, the court shall hold a hearing on the notice and, unless the court finds that one of the reasons set forth in subdivision (j) exists, shall order that the defendant be brought to trial within 10 days. A defendant not brought to trial within the 10-day period through no fault of the defendant, on motion of the defendant or the court, shall be forever discharged from the crime.

Another issue is that of **double jeopardy**. Article I, Section 9 of the Florida Constitution states that:

> No person shall be deprived of life, liberty or property without due process of law, or be twice put in jeopardy for the same offense...

Similarly, FS §910.11 states that:

(1) No person shall be held to answer on a second indictment, information, or affidavit for an offense for which the person has been acquitted. The acquittal shall be a bar to a subsequent prosecution for the same offense, notwithstanding any defect in the form or circumstances of the indictment, information, or affidavit.

(2) When a person may be tried for an offense in two or more counties, a conviction or acquittal in one county shall be a bar to prosecution for the same offense in another county.

The issue of double jeopardy may be grounds for the defense to make a pretrial motion to dismiss the case. Fla. R. Crim. P. 3.190(c) states that:

> ...the court may at any time entertain a motion to dismiss on any of the following grounds:
> (1) The defendant is charged with an offense for which the defendant has been pardoned.
> (2) The defendant is charged with an offense for which the defendant previously has been placed in jeopardy.
> (3) The defendant is charged with an offense for which the defendant previously has been granted immunity...

Innovative Defenses

There are a variety of relatively new **innovative defenses** against conviction. These include defenses such as the abuse defense, premenstrual syndrome, "black rage," and "urban survival syndrome." Most of these defenses are not discussed in the Florida Statutes or the Florida Rules of

Criminal Procedure. However, the **abuse defense** is known in Florida as the **Battered-Spouse Syndrome**. It is discussed in Fla. R. Crim. P. 3.201(a), which states that:

> When in any criminal case it shall be the intention of the defendant to rely on the defense of battered-spouse syndrome at trial, no evidence offered by the defendant for the purpose of establishing that defense shall be admitted in the case unless advance notice in writing of the defense shall have been given by the defendant...

For a defendant to use the battered-spouse defense, s/he is required by law to provide advance notice to the prosecution (similar to when the alibi or insanity defenses are used). Fla. R. Crim. P. 3.201(b) mandates pre-trial notification of intent to use the battered-spouse syndrome defense no less than 30 days prior to the trial. The requirement of notification falls solely on the defendant; the prosecution is not required to demand such notification.

SOURCES OF INFORMATION FOR LEGAL RESEARCH

Legal research involves the study of both statutes and case law from court decisions. Because the law is constantly changing, it is essential that only the most recent references be used. Today, much of the material may be found in electronic format: CD-ROMs and on-line computer databases such as WestLaw and Lexis have significantly streamlined legal research.

Legal Citations

Decisions of state appellate courts and the U.S. Supreme Court are published in books which are generally known as **reports** or **reporters**. A sample case citation is: *Assay v. State, 580 So.2d 610 (1991)*. In this particular case, the court defined premeditation as an element of first degree murder. *Assay v. State* is the name of the case; all cases that are heard in Florida courts are prosecuted in the name of the defendant versus "The State of Florida." The first number (580) represents the volume number in which the case is to be found. "So.2d" is an abbreviation for the specific reporter in which the case is to be found (*Southern Reporter, Second Series*). The second number (610) is the page number in the reporter on which the decision is to be found. The date in parentheses (1991) is the year in which the case was decided. Therefore, the above citation, 580 So.2d 610, which was decided in 1991, is found beginning on page 610 of volume 580 of the *Southern Reporter, Second Series*.

Statutory citations resemble case citations. A sample statutory citation is: **FS §782**. FS is an abbreviation for the Florida Statutes and the number 782 refers to the specific section number of the statute. This particular statute deals with the topic of homicide.

State and federal statutes use the following abbreviations:

- *United States Code* (USC) – contains the federal legal code, including the criminal code

- *Florida Statutes* (FS) – contains the legal code of the state of Florida, including the criminal code

- *Florida Rules of Criminal Procedure* (Fla. R. Crim. P.) – contains rules of evidence and matters pertaining to criminal procedure used in Florida

Court decisions are found in the following sources:

- *United States Reports* (US) – contains U.S. Supreme Court decisions

- *Supreme Court Reporter* (S.Ct) – contains U.S. Supreme Court decisions

- *Federal Reporter, 2nd series* (F.2d) – contains decisions from the Federal Court of Appeals

- *West's Southern Reporter, 2nd series* (So.2d) – contains decisions from courts in four southern states, including the Florida Supreme Court and the Florida District Courts of Appeal

- *Florida Reports* (Fla) – contains decisions from the Florida District Court of Appeal

- *Florida Supplement Second* (Fla. Supp. 2d) – contains decisions from both the Florida Circuit Courts and the Florida County Courts

Shepard's Citations

Shepard's Florida Citations, which is available on CD-ROM, contains an analysis of each appellate court decision. Each citation includes a history of the case, other decisions which cite this decision, and any other cases which have modified, overruled, or approved the decision. There are separate analyses for state statutes.

Other Sources of Information

There are a number of other sources of information on Florida law. However, it is important to remember that these sources are not official legal authorities.

A **legal digest** is a research tool that arranges issues by topic for easy reference. It allows a researcher studying a legal point from one case to easily find other court decisions which were made on similar issues. *West's Florida Digest, 2ⁿᵈ series* is one of the most popular legal digests for Florida. It indexes Florida's reported cases by both case name and subject.

Black's Law Dictionary is the most popular **legal dictionary** in America today and can be found in any law library. There are also several useful **legal encyclopedias** which discuss Florida state law and state legal issues. One of the most popular is *Florida Jurisprudence 2d*, which is an encyclopedia of Florida substantive law.

Law reviews are journals which contain scholarly legal research articles written by lawyers and law students. All the major law schools in Florida publish law reviews. Some of the major law reviews available in Florida include:

- *University of Miami Law Review* (U.Miami.L.Rev.)

- *Florida State University Law Review* (Fla. State L. Rev.)

- *University of Florida Law Review* (U.Fla.L.Rev.)

- *Stetson Law Review* (Stetson L.Rev.)

- *Nova Law Journal* (Nova L.J.)

Although law reviews are not legal authority, they are cited in the same way as court cases. For example, **15 U.Miami L.Rev. 392** would refer to an article beginning on page 392 of volume 15 of the *University of Miami Law Review*. This particular article deals with the issue of temporary insanity as a defense for the crime of homicide. Similarly, **7 Fla. State L.Rev. 729** would refer to an article beginning on page 729 of volume 7 of the *Florida State University Law Review*. This article deals with the issue of self-defense as a justifiable use of deadly force.

Other varied sources of information include the *Florida Bar Journal*, a monthly publication which is the official magazine for the Florida State Bar. *West's Florida Statutes Annotated*, which is published by West Publishing Company, contains the current laws of the state of Florida. The laws are annotated with case summaries, references to legal encyclopedias and law review articles, and short articles or practice commentaries which explain specific provisions. Finally, *West's Florida Law Finder* is a one-volume index to Florida cases, statutes, court rules, etc. It includes West Key numbers for easy reference to other West publications.

NOTES

1. The Florida Constitution and Statutes may be viewed online by going to the homepage of the Florida State Legislature (http://www.leg.state.fl.us/) and selecting the tab headed "Laws."
2. FS §775.012
3. FS §782.04
4. The five categories are listed in FS §775.081(1) and the associated penalties are outlined in FS §775.082.
5. FS §775.018(1)
6. The Florida Rules of Criminal Procedure may be viewed online on the homepage of the Florida Bar (http://www.flabar.org/). On the left side of the home page, click on "Links" and then on "Rules of Procedure."
7. FS §776.06(2)(a)
8. FS §794.021
9. *Florida Criminal Jury Instructions Handbook* (2002). Longwood, FL: Gould Publications, Inc., p.249.
10. *Zamora v. State*, 361 So.2d 776 (Fla. 3d DCA 1978)

CHAPTER 3

INDEX CRIMES

INTRODUCTION

The Federal Bureau of Investigation annually publishes the ***Uniform Crime Reports***[1] (UCR), the most widely used source of official data on crime and criminals in the United States. Much of the UCR deals with **index crimes**, a set of eight serious offenses that the FBI uses as a measure of crime in the United States. They are also known as **Part I Offenses** and include four violent crimes and four property crimes. The eight index crimes measured by the FBI are:

- homicide
- forcible rape
- robbery
- aggravated assault
- burglary
- larceny-theft
- motor-vehicle theft
- arson

However, the definitions used by the FBI in compiling the UCR are not always the same as those found in the Florida Statutes. This chapter will discuss in detail the definitions of these eight serious crimes as provided by Florida Statutes.

CRIMINAL HOMICIDE

Homicide is the killing of one human being by another. If that killing is illegal, then it is a form of **criminal homicide**. In Florida, criminal homicide is discussed in Chapter 782 of the Florida Statutes (FS) and includes the crimes of:

- murder (including first degree, second degree, and third degree)
- manslaughter
- vehicular or vessel homicide

In addition, Florida recognizes several categories of non-criminal homicide, including:

- justifiable homicide
- excusable homicide

All the criminal homicide offenses discussed in the Florid Statutes contain two key elements:

- conduct that causes the death of a person

- the mental culpability of the defendant

Essentially, the first of these elements is the guilty act (*actus reus*) and the second is the guilty mind (*mens rea*).

The specific homicide offense of which a defendant may be convicted depends on his or her level of mental culpability and on the nature of the circumstances surrounding the death (for example, the presence of aggravating factors).

First Degree Murder

First degree murder is defined in FS §782.04(1)(a), which states that:

The unlawful killing of a human being:

1. When perpetrated from a premeditated design to effect the death of the person killed or any human being;
2. When committed by a person engaged in the perpetration of, or in the attempt to perpetrate, any:
   a. Trafficking offense prohibited by s. 893.135(1),
   b. Arson,
   c. Sexual battery,
   d. Robbery,
   e. Burglary,
   f. Kidnapping,
   g. Escape,
   h. Aggravated child abuse,
   i. Aggravated abuse of an elderly person or disabled adult,
   j. Aircraft piracy,
   k. Unlawful throwing, placing, or discharging of a destructive device or bomb,
   l. Carjacking,
   m. Home-invasion robbery,
   n. Aggravated stalking,
   o. Murder of another human being,
   p. Resisting an officer with violence to his or her person;
   q. Felony that is an act of terrorism or is in furtherance of an act of terrorism; or
3. Which resulted from the unlawful distribution of any substance controlled under s. 893.03(1), cocaine ..., or opium or any synthetic or natural salt, compound, derivative, or preparation of opium by a person 18 years of age

or older, when such drug is proven to be the proximate cause of the death of the user,

is murder in the first degree and constitutes a capital felony...

The last element, relating to terrorism, was added to the statute after the terrorist attacks of September 11, 2001.

This statute identifies two specific categories of first degree murder: **premeditated murder** and **felony murder**. The first category involves the premeditated killing of another person. The Florida courts have defined premeditation as:

a fully formed conscious purpose to kill that may be formed in a moment and need only exist for such time as will allow the accused to be conscious of the nature of the act he is about to commit and the probable result of that act.[2]

The law does not define the amount of time that must pass between forming the premeditated idea of killing and the actual killing itself. It merely requires that the intent to kill be formed consciously before the killing takes place. However, while the courts have declined to set a precise amount of time that must pass between the formation of the specific intent to kill and the killing, they have held that some time must pass.[3]

To convict an offender of first degree premeditated murder, three elements must be proved beyond a reasonable doubt:

1. The victim is dead.

2. The death was caused by a criminal act on the part of the defendant.

3. The killing was premeditated.[4]

First degree felony murder, on the other hand, does not require that the offender had any premeditated intent to kill. However, it does require that the offender was engaged in one of a specified list of crimes and that death occurred as a consequence of, and while the offender was committing (or attempting to commit), that crime. If the death occurred while the offender was engaged in the commission of a crime that is not specifically listed in the statute, then the offender is not guilty of felony murder in the first degree, although s/he may be guilty of a lower degree of felony murder.

Murder in the first degree is a capital felony in Florida. According to FS §775.082(1):

A person who has been convicted of a capital felony shall be punished by death if the proceeding held to determine sentence ... results in findings by the court that such person shall be punished by death, otherwise such person shall be punished by life imprisonment and shall be ineligible for parole.

FS §921.141 discusses the proceedings for determining the sentence in a capital felony. It requires that, after the defendant is found guilty of a capital felony, a separate sentencing proceeding be held to determine whether the sentence will be death or life imprisonment. The hearing is held before a jury. If the defendant was found guilty through formal adjudication, the hearing is conducted by the trial judge before the trial jury. If the defendant pled guilty or waived his or her right to a jury trial, a jury will be impaneled for the sentencing proceeding. The jury hears evidence relating to possible aggravating and mitigating circumstances and then renders an advisory sentence to the judge, based upon:

(a) Whether sufficient aggravating circumstances exist...;
(b) Whether sufficient mitigating circumstances exist which outweigh the aggravating circumstances found to exist; and
(c) Based on these considerations, whether the defendant should be sentenced to life imprisonment or death.[5]

If the jury finds that the aggravating circumstances do not justify the imposition of the death penalty, or if the court feels that mitigating circumstances exist which outweigh the aggravating circumstances, the recommended sentence will be life imprisonment without possibility of parole. If the aggravating circumstances are sufficient and are not outweighed by the mitigating circumstances (if any), the recommended sentence will be death. The final sentencing decision rests with the judge and, if the sentence is death, it is subject to automatic review by the Florida Supreme Court.

Capital punishment in Florida is discussed in more detail in Chapter 7.

Second Degree Murder

Florida also recognizes both second degree murder and second degree felony murder. FS §782.04(2) defines **second degree murder** as:

> The unlawful killing of a human being, when perpetrated by any act imminently dangerous to another and evincing a depraved mind regardless of human life, although without any premeditated design to effect the death of any particular individual, is murder in the second degree and constitutes a felony of the first degree...

Second degree murder requires a "depraved mind." According to the courts,[6] this requires that the prosecution prove both that the killing was motivated by spite, hatred, or ill will and that the defendant showed indifference to human life. Specific intent to kill the victim is not required, just a general intent to commit an inherently dangerous act.[7]

In addition, FS 782.04(3) defines **second degree felony murder** as:

> When a person is killed in the perpetration of, or in the attempt to perpetrate, any:
> (a) Trafficking offense prohibited by s. 893.135(1),
> (b) Arson,

(c)　Sexual battery,

(d)　Robbery,

(e)　Burglary,

(f)　Kidnapping,

(g)　Escape,

(h)　Aggravated child abuse,

(i)　Aggravated abuse of an elderly person or disabled adult,

(j)　Aircraft piracy,

(k)　Unlawful throwing, placing, or discharging of a destructive device or bomb,

(l)　Carjacking,

(m)　Home-invasion robbery,

(n)　Aggravated stalking,

(o)　Murder of another human being,

(p)　Resisting an officer with violence to his or her person, or

(q)　Felony that is an act of terrorism or is in furtherance of an act of terrorism,

by a person other than the person engaged in the perpetration of or in the attempt to perpetrate such felony, the person perpetrating or attempting to perpetrate such felony is guilty of murder in the second degree...

For the crime to be felony murder, the killing must occur during the commission (or attempted commission) of one of the underlying crimes listed in the statute. If the killing occurs first and the underlying crime is committed as an afterthought, rather than having been intended from the start, felony murder has not been committed. Therefore, if the offender murders the victim and only then decides to steal the victim's wallet, the offender is not guilty of felony murder.

Both types of second degree murder are considered to be first degree felonies. They are punishable by "imprisonment for a term of years not exceeding life or as provided in s. 775.082, s. 775.083, or s. 775.084."[8]

Third Degree Felony Murder

Florida recognizes a category of felony murder known as **third degree felony murder**. This is defined in FS §782.04(4) as:

> The unlawful killing of a human being, when perpetrated without any design to effect death, by a person engaged in the perpetration of, or in the attempt to perpetrate, any felony other than any:
>
> (a)　Trafficking offense prohibited by s. 893.135(1),
>
> (b)　Arson,
>
> (c)　Sexual battery,
>
> (d)　Robbery,
>
> (e)　Burglary,
>
> (f)　Kidnapping,
>
> (g)　Escape,
>
> (h)　Aggravated child abuse,

(i)   Aggravated abuse of an elderly person or disabled adult,

(j)   Aircraft piracy,

(k)   Unlawful throwing, placing, or discharging of a destructive device or bomb,

(l)   Unlawful distribution of any substance controlled under s. 893.03(1), cocaine as described in s. 893.03(2)(a)4., or opium or any synthetic or natural salt, compound, derivative, or preparation of opium by a person 18 years of age or older, when such drug is proven to be the proximate cause of the death of the user,

(m)   Carjacking,

(n)   Home-invasion robbery,

(o)   Aggravated stalking,

(p)   Murder of another human being,

(q)   Resisting an officer with violence to his or her person, or

(r)   Felony that is an act of terrorism or is in furtherance of an act of terrorism

is murder in the third degree and constitutes a felony of the second degree, punishable as provided in s. 775.082, s. 775.083, or s. 775.084.

For an offender to be convicted of this crime, it is not necessary for the prosecution to prove that the death was intended, only that it happened during the commission of one of the felonies listed in the statute. As with more serious levels of felony murder, all elements of the underlying felony must be proved or the offender cannot be convicted of felony murder.

Manslaughter

FS §782.07(1) defines **manslaughter** as:

> The killing of a human being by the act, procurement, or culpable negligence of another, without lawful justification ... and in cases in which such killing shall not be excusable homicide or murder ... is manslaughter..

Essentially, the crime includes two elements to convict an offender of manslaughter:

1. The victim is dead.

2. The defendant intentionally caused the death of the victim, intentionally procured the death of the victim, or caused the victim's death by culpable negligence.

In addition, the killing must not be justified or be an excusable homicide.[9]

The *Florida* **Criminal Jury Instructions Handbook** defines culpable negligence as:

> ...consciously doing an act or following a course of conduct that the defendant must have known, or reasonably should have known, was likely to cause death or great bodily injury.[10]

In most cases, manslaughter is a second degree felony. However, if the victim is an elderly person, a disabled adult, or an individual under the age of 18, and death was caused by culpable negligence, the crime becomes a first degree felony.

Vehicular and Vessel Homicide

Florida state law has separate statutes that specifically cover criminal homicide that was caused by the operation of a motor vehicle or a vessel of some type. FS §782.071 defines **vehicular homicide** as:

> ...the killing of a human being ... caused by the operation of a motor vehicle by another in a reckless manner likely to cause the death of, or great bodily harm to, another.

In most cases, vehicular homicide is a second degree felony. However, if the offender was aware of the accident and fails to give information and render aid to the victim, the crime becomes a first degree felony. This is true even if the offender did not know that the accident actually resulted in injury or death.

Vessel homicide is defined in FS §782.072 as:

> ...the killing of a human being by the operation of a vessel ... by another in a reckless manner likely to cause the death of, or great bodily harm to, another.

A vessel is defined is FS §372.02 as being synonymous with boat and includes any watercraft (other than a seaplane on the water) which may be used for transportation on the water. In most cases, vessel homicide is a second degree felony. However, as with vehicular homicide, if at the time of the accident the offender knew that it had occurred and failed to give information or render aid to the victim, the crime becomes a first degree felony, even if the offender did not know that the accident resulted in injury or death to the victim.

These crimes include the element of reckless driving. Therefore, under double jeopardy, a defendant cannot be convicted of both vehicular homicide and reckless driving.[11]

Non-Criminal Homicide

Although the UCR focuses specifically on criminal homicide, there are situations when the killing of one human being by another is lawful and therefore not a crime. Non-criminal homicides may be justifiable or excusable.

Excusable homicide is a death that is caused by an accident or other misfortune, when no unlawful intent is involved in the act that caused the death. FS §782.03 defines excusable homicide, stating that:

Homicide is excusable when committed by accident and misfortune in doing any lawful act by lawful means with usual ordinary caution, and without any unlawful intent, or by accident and misfortune in the heat of passion, upon any sudden and sufficient provocation, or upon a sudden combat, without any dangerous weapon being used and not done in a cruel or unusual manner.

An automobile accident that does not involve negligence or any unlawful act on the part of the driver is an example of excusable homicide.

Justifiable homicide is a killing that was committed with the use of justifiable deadly force. Justifiable homicide is defined in FS §782.02, which states that:

The use of deadly force is justifiable when a person is resisting any attempt to murder such person or to commit any felony upon him or her or upon or in any dwelling house in which such person shall be.

Essentially, justifiable homicide is a form of self-defense. The courts have stated that an individual may use deadly force to defend himself or herself only if s/he has a reasonable belief that deadly force is necessary to protect the individual or his or her dwelling.[12] In addition, for an individual to claim justifiable homicide, s/he cannot have been the initial aggressor. Some force must have been used on the defendant first before s/he has the privilege of using force against the aggressor.

Because justifiable and excusable homicides are not criminal acts, there are no punishments associated with these acts.

FORCIBLE RAPE/SEXUAL BATTERY

In the Uniform Crime Reporting Program, **forcible rape** is defined as "the carnal knowledge of a female forcibly and against her will."[13] In Florida, the crime of rape has been replaced with that of **sexual battery**, which is discussed in Chapter 794 of the Florida Statutes. This crime is gender-neutral as the statutes do not specify the gender of either the offender or the victim. Therefore, in Florida, either a male or female offender may be convicted of the sexual battery of either a male or female victim. Unlike some states, the statutes do allow for same-sex sexual battery.[14] In addition, actual sexual gratification is not an element of any type of sexual battery.[15]

Sexual battery is defined in FS §794.011(1)(h) as:

...oral, anal, or vaginal penetration by, or union with, the sexual organ of another or the anal or vaginal penetration of another by any other object; however, sexual battery does not include an act done for a bona fide medical purpose.

When the crime involves the use of an object other than a sexual organ, some penetration, however slight, must be shown. However, when the crime involves the sexual organ of another individual, contact or union is sufficient.

All of the sexual battery crimes in Florida require that the act be committed without the victim's consent. Consent, according to FS §794.011(1)(a),

> ...means intelligent, knowing, and voluntary consent and does not include coerced submission. "Consent" shall not be deemed or construed to mean the failure by the alleged victim to offer physical resistance to the offender.

Therefore, it is not necessary for the victim to resist physically for the act to be a crime. If the victim chooses to submit to the offender (for example, to avoid additional physical injury), this does not mean that the victim has consented to the sexual act.

FS §794.011(5) discusses the least serious sexual battery offense:

> A person who commits sexual battery upon a person 12 years of age or older, without that person's consent, and in the process thereof does not use physical force and violence likely to cause serious personal injury.

This is the basic charge of sexual battery and is a necessary included offense for the more serious sexual battery offenses which are outlined in other sections of this statute. This crime is a second degree felony. However, if the victim was **gang raped** — in other words, more than one offender committed sexual battery upon the victim during the same criminal event — it is reclassified to a first degree felony.[16]

The next level of sexual battery is a first degree felony. It is defined in FS 794.011(4) as:

> A person who commits sexual battery upon a person 12 years of age or older without that person's consent, under any of the following circumstances...:
> (a) When the victim is physically helpless to resist.
> (b) When the offender coerces the victim to submit by threatening to use force or violence likely to cause serious personal injury on the victim, and the victim reasonably believes that the offender has the present ability to execute the threat.
> (c) When the offender coerces the victim to submit by threatening to retaliate against the victim, or any other person, and the victim reasonably believes that the offender has the ability to execute the threat in the future.
> (d) When the offender, without the prior knowledge or consent of the victim, administers or has knowledge of someone else administering to the victim any narcotic, anesthetic, or other intoxicating substance which mentally or physically incapacitates the victim.

(e) When the victim is mentally defective and the offender has reason to believe this or has actual knowledge of this fact.

(f) When the victim is physically incapacitated.

(g) When the offender is a law enforcement officer, correctional officer, or correctional probation officer ... or is an elected official..., or any other person in a position of control or authority in a probation, community control, controlled release, detention, custodial, or similar setting, and such officer, official, or person is acting in such a manner as to lead the victim to reasonably believe that the offender is in a position of control or authority as an agent or employee of government.

Again, if there are multiple offenders committing acts of sexual battery upon the victim during the same criminal event, the crime is reclassified from a first degree felony to a life felony.[17]

FS §794.011(3) defines the next type of sexual battery as:

...a person who commits sexual battery upon a person 12 years of age or older, without that person's consent, and in the process thereof uses or threatens to use a deadly weapon or uses actual physical force likely to cause serious personal injury...

The key difference between this offense and that defined in FS §794.011(5) is the presence of physical force or the use or threat of a deadly weapon. However, battery and sexual battery as defined in FS §794.011(5) are necessarily included offenses. This crime is a life felony.

Finally, FS §794.011(2) outlines the most serious type of sexual battery in Florida, that committed upon an individual who is less than 12 years of age:

(a) A person 18 years of age or older who commits sexual battery upon, or in an attempt to commit sexual battery injures the sexual organs of, a person less than 12 years of age commits a capital felony...

(b) A person less than 18 years of age who commits sexual battery upon, or in an attempt to commit sexual battery injures the sexual organs of, a person less than 12 years of age commits a life felony...

For this crime, the victim must be less than 12 years of age. The courts have ruled that an individual who was victimized on her birthday was not a victim under the age of 12 for the purposes of this crime.[18]

Unlike other types of sexual battery, for this offense the age of the offender determines the relative seriousness of the crime. If the offender is under 18 years of age, the crime is a life felony. If s/he is at least 18 years of age, the crime is a capital felony.

ROBBERY

The Uniform Crime Reporting Program defines **robbery** as "the taking or attempting to take anything of value from the care, custody, or control of a person or persons by force or threat of force or violence and/or by putting the victim in fear."[19] In Florida, FS §812.13(1) defines robbery as:

> ...the taking of money or other property which may be the subject of larceny from the person or custody of another, with intent to either permanently or temporarily deprive the person or the owner of the money or other property, when in the course of the taking there is the use of force, violence, assault, or putting in fear.

Essentially, robbery in Florida has three elements:

1. The offender commits a larceny by taking the property from the victim or the custody of the victim.

2. The defendant uses or threatens to use physical force upon another person or place that person in fear.

3. The defendant's intent is to take or retain the property of another person either permanently or temporarily.

This definition presents robbery as a theft in which the property is taken from the immediate presence or control of the victim and against the victim's will, using force or the threat of force. This element of force is what distinguishes robbery from theft. Because of the use of force or fear to illegally acquire personal property, Florida considers robbery to be both a crime against the person and a crime against property.

The person who is robbed does not have to be the actual owner of the property. If s/he has custody of the property at the time of the crime, the element of larceny is still met.

Actual force or violence is not required in the crime of robbery. A threat that places the victim in fear is sufficient. The victim is not required by law to have resisted physically in any way if resistence would place the victim in fear of death or great bodily harm. However, if the victim was not prevented from resisting by fear, there must be some resistance so that the taking was done by force or violence. Essentially, either force or fear is sufficient to meet the requirement outlined in the definition above, but one or the other is necessary. The statute does not define the means by which the force is used or fear is imposed. However, the courts have stated that the amount of force used must be greater than that necessary to simply seize the property from the victim.[20]

Because the element of larceny is a requirement for the crime of robbery, if no property is actually taken, the defendant cannot be found guilty of robbery. In addition, for the charge of attempted robbery, intent to take property must be established. However, even if it cannot be shown that the defendant took or intended to take property, s/he may be guilty of assault or some other crime.

If the offender carried a firearm or some other deadly weapon while committing the robbery, the crime is a first degree felony. If the offender carried some other weapon, the crime is also a first degree felony. If the offender carried no weapon of any kind (deadly or non-deadly) during the commission of the robbery, it is a second degree felony.

Recently, Florida codified the crime of **carjacking,** which is a form of robbery. FS §812.133(1) defines carjacking as:

> ...the taking of a motor vehicle which may be the subject of larceny from the person or custody of another, with intent to either permanently or temporarily deprive the person or the owner of the motor vehicle, when in the course of the taking there is the use of force, violence, assault, or putting in fear.

Essentially, carjacking involves robbing the victim of a motor vehicle. The victim does not need to be the owner of the vehicle, only to have custody of the vehicle at the time of the crime. The requirements regarding force and fear, and the victim's resistance to the crime, are the same as for robbery.

ASSAULT AND BATTERY

There is often some confusion about the actual meaning of **assault**. Although many people believe that assault involves inflicting an injury upon another person, in reality, this is not the case. An assault is an intentional attempt or threat to cause injury. If the injury is actually inflicted, a **battery** has occurred. The *Uniform Crime Reporting Program* focuses specifically on aggravated assault, which it defines as:

> an unlawful attack by one person upon another for the purpose of inflicting severe or aggravated bodily injury. This type of assault is usually accompanied by the use of a weapon or by means likely to produce death or great bodily harm.[21]

In Florida, assault is defined in FS §784.011 as:

> ...an intentional, unlawful threat by word or act to do violence to the person of another, coupled with an apparent ability to do so, and doing some act which creates a well-founded fear in such other person that such violence is imminent.

Simple assault is a second degree misdemeanor in Florida. An **aggravated assault**, which is discussed in FS §784.021, is an assault that was either made with a deadly weapon (but without any intent to kill) or with a conscious intent to commit a felony. Aggravated assault is a third degree felony.

According to FS §784.03(1)(a), the crime of battery occurs when an offender:

1. Actually and intentionally touches or strikes another person against the will of the other; or
2. Intentionally causes bodily harm to another person.

Simple battery is a first degree misdemeanor in Florida. The crime becomes **felony battery** when one of the following conditions is met:

1. The harm caused to the victim is great bodily harm, permanent disability, or permanent disfigurement (discussed in FS §784.041); or

2. The offender committing the battery has two prior convictions for battery (discussed in FS §784.03(2)).

Aggravated battery occurs when the offender, while committing a battery:

1. Intentionally or knowingly causes great bodily harm, permanent disability, or permanent disfigurement; or
2. Uses a deadly weapon.[22]

In addition, if the victim was pregnant at the time of the crime and the offender either knew or should have known of the pregnancy, the crime is also one of aggravated battery. Felony battery is a third degree felony; aggravated battery is a felony of the second degree.

Essentially, an assault is an attempted battery. Therefore, there is no crime of attempted assault in Florida. There is a crime known as attempted aggravated battery, but the courts have stated that there is little difference between an attempted aggravated battery and an aggravated assault.[23]

An assault or battery directed against certain public officials (including law enforcement officers, firefighters, emergency medical care providers, or public transit employees or agents) is discussed separately in FS §784.07. Essentially, it is an aggravating factor if the public official who was victimized was engaged in the lawful performance of his or her duties at the time of the crime. In this situation, the offense is reclassified to be more serious, as follows:

- assault becomes a first degree misdemeanor

- battery becomes a third degree felony

- aggravated assault becomes a second degree felony; if the victim was a law enforcement officer, the statute also states that the offender must receive a minimum term of three years imprisonment

- aggravated battery is increased to a first degree felony and, if the victim was a law enforcement officer, the offender must receive a minimum term of imprisonment of five years

In addition, the offender may not have the adjudication of guilt or imposition of sentence suspended or deferred. This makes him or her ineligible for any type of pretrial diversion program. The offender also is not eligible for any discretionary early release or statutory gain time (other than a pardon, executive clemency, or conditional medical release) before s/he has served the minimum sentence.

In addition to public officials, there are other categories of victims which result in statutory increases in the minimum penalty for assault or battery. These include:

- health services personnel[24]
- victims 65 years of age or older[25]
- elected officials, employees of schools, and employees of the Department of Children and Family Services[26]
- code inspectors[27]

BURGLARY

In common law, the crime of **burglary** was defined as the breaking and entering of a dwelling at night with intent to commit a felony. Today, the definition of burglary includes structures other than a dwelling place, can occur during the daytime as well as at night, and can involve either an intended felony or misdemeanor. The UCR defines burglary as the "unlawful entry of a structure to commit a felony or theft."[28]

The definition of burglary in the Florida Statutes was revised in 2001. According to FS §810.02(1)(b):

> For offenses committed after July 1, 2001, "burglary" means:
> 1. Entering or remaining in a dwelling, a structure, or a conveyance with the intent to commit an offense therein, unless the premises are at the time open to the public or the defendant is licensed or invited to enter; or
> 2. Notwithstanding a licensed or invited entry, remaining in a dwelling, structure, or conveyance;
>   a. Surreptitiously, with the intent to commit an offense therein;
>   b. After permission to remain therein has been withdrawn, with the intent to commit an offense therein; or
>   c. To commit or attempt to commit a forcible felony...

Basically, a burglary occurs when an offender unlawfully enters one of the locations defined by statute with a felonious intent. In Florida, the crime of burglary is completed when the offender enters the building, regardless of whether the offense intended to be committed within the structure was actually carried out. While the crime requires entry, forcible entry or "breaking" is not required. Any form of entry with intent is enough to meet the element of entry required for the crime of burglary. In some situations, a burglary may even occur if the owner of the building invited the offender *into the building or in some other way gave the offender permission to enter.* The permission to enter is canceled or nullified by the criminal intent of the burglar. Therefore, if an individual enters the location at a time when it was open to the public (e.g., entering a shop during regular business hours) but remains within after s/he knew that the premises were closed to the public, s/he may be guilty of burglary. In addition, if the offender is in a location that is open to the public but enters or remains in areas of that location that s/he knew or should have known were not open to the public, s/he may be guilty of burglary. However, an individual cannot be found guilty of burglarizing his or her own property, *as s/he has the legal right to enter the premises.*

The requirement of entry (dwelling, structure, or conveyance) does not mean that the offender's entire body must inside the location. If the offender extended any part of his or her body far enough into the location to commit the intended offense, thus breaking the airspace of the location, the element of the crime is considered to have been met. For example, the courts have held that reaching into the open bed of a pick-up truck is sufficient to be considered as partial entry.[29] However, *if an item falls out of the truck and is picked up from the street by an individual who did not actually enter the truck with any part of his or her body or with any instrument,* the element of entry was not met and the individual is not guilty of the crime of burglary.[30]

FS §810.011 defines many of the key terms used in the definition of burglary. A **structure** is any temporary or permanent building which has a roof. A **dwelling** is any type of building or conveyance which has a roof and which is designed to be occupied by people who live within it. *It may be either temporary or permanent and the definition includes both mobile and immobile dwellings.* The curtilage or space of ground immediately around the structure or dwelling is also included in the definition. A **conveyance** includes motor vehicles, ships, vessels, railroad car, trailer, aircraft, or sleeping car.

The circumstances surrounding the offense determine its level of seriousness. There are a number of aggravating circumstances which increase the punishment for burglary. According to FS §810.02(2), burglary is considered a first degree felony if, while committing the offense, the offender:

(a) Makes an assault or battery upon any person; or
(b) Is or becomes armed within the dwelling, structure, or conveyance, with explosives or a dangerous weapon; or
(c) Enters an occupied or unoccupied dwelling or structure, and:
1. Uses a motor vehicle as an instrumentality, other than merely as a getaway vehicle, to assist in committing the offense, and thereby damages the dwelling or structure; or
2. Causes damage to the dwelling or structure, or to property within the dwelling or structure in excess of $1,000.

According to FS §810.02(3), burglary is a second degree felony if:

> ...in the course of committing the offense, the offender does not make an assault or battery and is not and does not become armed with a dangerous weapon or explosive, and the offender enters or remains in a:
> (a) Dwelling, and there is another person in the dwelling at the time the offender enters or remains;
> (b) Dwelling, and there is not another person in the dwelling at the time the offender enters or remains;
> (c) Structure, and there is another person in the structure at the time the offender enters or remains; or
> (d) Conveyance, and there is another person in the conveyance at the time the offender enters or remains.

Finally, according to FS §810.02(4), burglary is a third degree felony if:

> ...in the course of committing the offense, the offender does not make an assault or battery and is not and does not become armed with a dangerous weapon or explosive, and the offender enters or remains in a:
> (a) Structure, and there is not another person in the structure at the time the offender enters or remains; or
> (b) Conveyance, and there is not another person in the conveyance at the time the offender enters or remains.

LARCENY-THEFT

The FBI defines **larceny-theft** as:

> the unlawful taking, carrying, leading, or riding away of property from the possession or constructive possession of another. It includes crimes such as shoplifting, pocket-picking, purse-snatching, thefts from motor vehicles, thefts of motor vehicle parts and accessories, bicycle thefts, etc., in which no use of force, violence, or fraud occurs.[31]

In Florida, the equivalent crime is known simply as **theft**. FS §812.014(1) states that:

> A person commits theft if he or she knowingly obtains or uses, or endeavors to obtain or to use, the property of another with intent to, either temporarily or permanently:
> (a) Deprive the other person of a right to the property or a benefit from the property.
> (b) Appropriate the property to his or her own use or to the use of any person not entitled to the use of the property.

In Florida, theft is a specific intent crime. Thus, the offender must have had the intent to steal prior to committing the actual theft.[32] Even if the personal property stolen is something that is unlawful to possess, such as illegal drugs, the offender could still be convicted of the crime of theft. FS §812.012(4) defines **property** as anything of value, including:

- real property (including the physical contents of land, such as items in the land or growing on the land)

- personal property, both tangible and intangible

- services (including anything of value which results from an individual's labor or skill, either physical or mental, or from the use or possession of property)

Florida recognizes several levels of theft. **Grand theft in the first degree** is defined in FS §812.014(2)(a) and requires the following conditions:

1. If the property stolen is valued at $100,000 or more; or
2. If the property stolen is cargo valued at $50,000 or more...; or
3. If the offender commits any grand theft and:
   a. In the course of committing the offense the offender uses a motor vehicle as an instrumentality, other than merely as a getaway vehicle, to assist in committing the offense and thereby damages the real property of another; or
   b. In the course of committing the offense the offender causes damage to the real or personal property of another in excess of $1,000...

This crime is a first degree felony.

Grand theft in the second degree, which is a second degree felony, is defined in FS §812.014(2)(b) and requires the following conditions:

1. ...the property stolen is valued at $20,000 or more, but less than $100,000;
2. The property stolen is cargo valued at less than $50,000...; or
3. The property stolen is emergency medical equipment valued at $300 or more...

Grand theft in the third degree, a third degree felony, is determined by the value or type of property stolen. According to FS §812.014(2)(c), third degree grand theft occurs if the property that has been stolen is:

1. Valued at $300 or more, but less than $5,000.
2. Valued at $5,000 or more, but less than $10,000.
3. Valued at $10,000 or more, but less than $20,000.
4. A will, codicil, or other testamentary instrument.
5. A firearm.
6. A motor vehicle...
7. Any commercially farmed animal...
8. Any fire extinguisher.

43

9. Any amount of citrus fruit consisting of 2,000 or more individual pieces of fruit.
10. Taken from a designated construction site identified by the posting of a sign...
11. Any stop sign.

In addition, according to FS §812.014(2)(d),

> It is grand theft of the third degree and a felony of the third degree ... if the property stolen is valued at $100 or more, but less than $300, and is taken from a dwelling ... or from the unenclosed curtilage of a dwelling...

Clearly, the specific charge of theft frequently depends on the actual value of the property that was stolen. FS §812.012(10) discusses how the value of property is determined. In most cases, the statute defines value as:

> ...the market value of the property at the time and place of the offense or, if such cannot be satisfactorily ascertained, the cost of replacement of the property within a reasonable time after the offense.[33]

However, for some items, such as written instruments, the market value may not be easy to determine. Therefore, FS §812.012(10)(a)2 states that written instruments such as checks, drafts, and promissory notes, are generally valued at face value (i.e., the amount due) and other instruments are valued based upon the economic loss suffered by the owner. If the stolen property is a trade secret which does not have a market value that can be readily determined, the value set upon it is "any reasonable value representing the damage to the owner, suffered by reason of losing an advantage over those who do not know of or use the trade secret."[34] Finally, if the minimum value of the property cannot be determined based on this statute, FS §812.012(10)(b) states that the value shall be held to be less than $100.

MOTOR VEHICLE THEFT

The UCR considers **motor vehicle theft** to be a separate index crime from that of theft or larceny-theft. It is defined by the FBI as:

> the theft or attempted theft of a motor vehicle, this offense category includes the stealing of automobiles, trucks, buses, motorcycles, motorscooters, snowmobiles, etc.[35]

While Florida does not consider motor vehicle theft to be a separate crime, there are several crimes outlined in the Florida Statutes which correspond to this index crime. The statutory definition of grand theft in the third degree, which is found in FS §812.014(2)(c), specifically includes the theft of a motor vehicle. However, it is necessary to prove that the offender intended to permanently defraud the owner of the property to convict an offender of grand theft under this statute, and it may be difficult to prove such intent. In addition, carjacking is defined in FS §812.133 (see the discussion

44

under **Robbery** earlier in this chapter) and does involve the taking of a motor vehicle from another's person or custody. In Florida, carjacking is considered to be a form of robbery rather than a theft.

ARSON

Like burglary, the common-law felony crime of **arson** was a crime against a home or dwelling place. While it could occur at any time of day, nighttime arson was considered to be a more serious crime. The UCR defines arson as:

> any willful or malicious burning or attempt to burn, with or without intent to defraud, a dwelling house, public building, motor vehicle or aircraft, personal property of another, etc.[36]

Today, Florida law recognizes arson against structures other than a home, as well as the burning of other types of property. There are two levels of arson outlined in the Florida Statutes, **first degree arson** and **second degree arson**.

First degree arson is defined in FS §806.01(1), which states that:

> Any person who willfully and unlawfully, or while in the commission of any felony, by fire or explosion, damages or causes to be damaged:
> (a)   Any dwelling, whether occupied or not, or its contents;
> (b)   Any structure, or contents thereof, where persons are normally present, such as: jails, prisons, or detention centers; hospitals, nursing homes, or other health care facilities; department stores, office buildings, business establishments, churches, or educational institutions during normal hours of occupancy; or other similar structures; or
> (c)   Any other structure that he or she knew or had reasonable grounds to believe was occupied by a human being,
> is guilty of arson in the first degree, which constitutes a felony of the first degree...

A structure includes any of the following, according to FS §806.01(3):

- any type of building
- any area that is enclosed and has a roof over it
- any real property and its appurtenances
- any tent or portable building
- any vehicle
- any vessel
- any watercraft
- any aircraft

Even if a building is temporarily unoccupied, it may still qualify as a dwelling if the period of unoccupancy is temporary or if it appears that when the occupants of the building left, they intended to return and resume residence in the building.

FS §806.01(2) defines second degree arson, which is a second degree felony, as the following:

> Any person who willfully and unlawfully, or while in the commission of any felony, by fire or explosion, damages or causes to be damaged any structure, whether the property of himself or herself or another, under any circumstances not referred to in subsection (1), is guilty of arson in the second degree...

Intent is required for arson; a fire that is of accidental or unintentional origin is not considered to be arson. If a person burns his or her own personal property, it may still be arson if the damaged property was an occupied structure or if the property was damaged by fire during the commission of a felony. In addition, FS §817.233 discusses the crime of burning to defraud the insurer. This statute states that:

> Any person who willfully and with intent to injure or defraud the insurer sets fire to or burns or attempts so to do or who causes to be burned or who aids, counsels or procures the burning of any building, structure or personal property, of whatsoever class or character, whether the property of himself or herself or of another, which shall at the time be insured by any person against loss or damage by fire, shall be guilty of a felony of the third degree...

HATE CRIMES

Hate or bias crimes are not specifically included among the UCR's eight index crimes. However, the FBI began to collect data on this category of crime after President Bush signed the Hate Crimes Statistics Act in 1990. The UCR defines hate or bias crimes as "those offenses motivated in part or singularly by personal prejudice against others because of a diversity—race, sexual orientation, religion, ethnicity/national origin, or disability.[37]

The Florida Attorney General's Office defines a hate crime as:

> an act committed or attempted by one person or group against another, or their property, that in any way constitutes an expression of hatred toward the victim based on his or her personal characteristics. It is a crime in which the perpetrator intentionally selects the victim based on one of the following characteristics: race, color, religion, ethnicity, ancestry, national origin, sexual orientation, mental or physical disability, or advanced age.[23]

In 1989, the Florida State Legislature enacted a number of state statutes which focus specifically on hate crimes. FS §775.085 enhances the penalty for hate-based criminal actions, stating that:

> The penalty for any felony or misdemeanor shall be reclassified as provided in this subsection if the commission of such felony or misdemeanor evidences prejudice based on the race, color, ancestry, ethnicity, religion, sexual orientation, national origin, mental or physical disability, or advanced age of the victim...

FS §877.19 is entitled "Hate Crimes Reporting Act" and requires all law enforcement agencies in the state to make monthly reports of hate crimes to the Florida Department of Law Enforcement (FDLE). The State Attorney General is required to publish an annual summary of the data collected by the FDLE. It is interesting to note that, in Florida, elements such as the victim's physical or mental disability or advanced age are also covered by the hate crimes law. However, although these elements were added to the law in 1998, the Legislature did not amend the Hate Crimes Reporting Act to include these elements. Because of this, law enforcement agencies are not required to keep records on hate crimes that involve victims with a mental or physical disability, or who are of an advanced age. Similarly, the Attorney General's annual report does not include this information.

There were a total of 306 hate crimes in Florida during 2002. Of these, 72 percent were crimes against persons, such as murder, robbery, and assault, while the remaining 28 percent were property crimes such as burglary, arson, and vandalism. The most common violent hate crime was assault; approximately 51 percent of all reported hate crimes in Florida were simple or aggravated assaults. The most common property hate crime was vandalism, comprising almost 25 percent of all reported hate crimes in the state.[38]

The most frequent motivation was the race or color of the victim; almost 53 percent of the 306 reported hate crimes were motivated by the victim's race or color. Other motivations included the victim's sexual orientation (18 percent), religion (13 percent), and ethnicity or national origin (14 percent). Since the state began keeping detailed statistics in 1991, race has always been the most prevalent motivator for hate crimes. However, the 2001 data on hate crimes in Florida showed a significant increase in hate crimes motivated by the religion and/or ethnicity of the victim. The Attorney General's Office attributed this change to the terrorist attacks on September 11, 2001. In 2002, the total number of reported hate crimes decreased from the 2001 figure of 335 and the percentage of crimes motivated by religion or ethnicity decreased to pre-2001 levels.[39]

NOTES

1.	Recent issues of the *Uniform Crime Reports* may be viewed online on the Federal Bureau of Investigation's website (http://www.fbi.gov/ucr/ucr.htm)
2.	*Assay v. State*, 580 So.2d 610 (Fla. 1991)
3.	*Weaver v. State*, 200 So.2d 53 (Fla. 2d DCA 1969)

4.   *Florida Criminal Jury Instructions Handbook* (2002). Longwood, FL: Gould Publications, Inc.

5.   FS 921.141(2)

6.   *Davis v. State*, 397 So.2d 1005 (Fla. 1st DCA 1981)

7.   *Conyers v. State*, 569 So.2d 1360 (Fla. 1st DCA 1990)

8.   FS §782.04(3)

9.   *State v. Richards*, 639 So.2d 680 (Fla. 2d DCA 1994)

10.   *Florida Criminal Jury Instructions Handbook, op cit.*, p.44

11.   *Norstrom v. State*, 616 So.2d 592 (Fla. 4th DCA 1993)

12.   *Lusk v. State*, 531 So.2d 1377(Fla. 2d DCA 1988)

13.   *Uniform Crime Reports, op cit.*

14.   *State v. Pate*, 656 So.2d 1323 (Fla. 5th DCA 1995)

15.   *State v. Rider*, 449 So.2d 903 (Fla. 3d Dist, 1984)

16.   FS §794.023(2)

17.   *Ibid*

18.   *Velasquez v. State*, 648 So.2d 302 (Fla. 5th DCA 1995)

19.   *Uniform Crime Reports, op cit.*

20.   *Robinson v. State*, 692 So.2d 833 (Fla. 1997)

21.   *Uniform Crime Reports, op cit.*

22.   FS §784.045(1)(a)

23.   *Henderson v. State* 370 So.2d 435 (Fla. 1st DCA 1979)

24.   See FS §784.076

25.   See FS §784.08

26.   See FS §784.081

27.   See FS §784.083

28.   *Uniform Crime Reports, op cit.*

29.   *Braswell v. State*, 671 So.2d 228 (Fla. 1st DCA 1996)

30.   *Acuzy v. State*, 705 So.2d 129 (Fla. 3d DCA 1998)

31.   *Uniform Crime Reports, op cit.*

32.   *Iglesias v. State*, 676 So.2d 75 (Fla. 3d DCA 1996)

33.   FS 812.012(10)(a)1

34.   FS 812.012(10)(a)3

35.   *Uniform Crime Reports, op cit.*

36.   *Ibid*

37.   Recent issues of the FBI's *Hate Crime Statistics* may be viewed online on the FBI's website (http://www.fbi.gov/ucr/ucr.htm)

38.   *Hate Crimes in Florida, January 1, 2002 - December 31, 2002* (http://myfloridalegal.com/02hate.pdf)

CHAPTER 4

THE POLICE IN FLORIDA

INTRODUCTION

There are many levels of police agencies in America today, including federal law enforcement, state police, county sheriff's agencies, and city police. There are over 400 separate law enforcement agencies in Florida today. Most of these are municipal departments. In addition, there are 67 county sheriff's departments, one state police agency (the Florida Highway Patrol), and a wide variety of special-purpose law enforcement agencies at all levels of government. Currently, there are over 38,000 full-time sworn law enforcement officers working in various agencies in Florida. Of these, almost 87 percent are male and over 77 percent are white.[1]

Florida's location on the Atlantic Ocean and the Gulf of Mexico creates a number of special law enforcement problems, including issues such as drugs, immigration, and tourism. Because of this, a large number of federal law enforcement agencies have offices in Florida and/or are involved in law enforcement activities within the state. This includes the Federal Bureau of Investigation, the Drug Enforcement Agency, the Immigration and Naturalization Service, U.S. Customs, the Bureau of Alcohol, Tobacco, and Firearms, the U.S. Coast Guard, and the U.S. Border Patrol. This results in a considerable amount of overlap among the various levels of law enforcement in the state.

LOCAL POLICING

The majority of the police departments in Florida are local or city departments. Currently, there are 288 local police agencies in the state. Generally, the chief or director of each department is appointed by the head of the city's political system (city manager, mayor, commissioner, etc.) Every local department is independent of every other department. The goals, purposes, and priorities vary greatly among departments, with each local agency responding to the needs and desires of the population it serves. All municipal police departments are full-service police agencies which provide a wide range of police services, including law enforcement, order maintenance, and service.

According to the Florida Department of Law Enforcement, as of June, 2002, a total of 16,266 sworn officers were employed in local police departments in Florida. Of these, approximately 87 percent were male and 13 percent female. Approximately 76 percent were white, 13 percent Hispanic, 10 percent black, and 1 percent of other races. The largest local police department in Florida is the Miami Police Department, with 1,070 sworn officers, followed by the Tampa Police Department with 969 sworn officers. In contrast, there are a considerable number of local departments with less than ten sworn officers.[2]

The Fort Lauderdale Police Department

The City of Fort Lauderdale, which is in Miami-Dade County, was incorporated in 1911. That same year, the first city marshal was appointed. The first **Fort Lauderdale Police Department (FLPD)** officer earned a salary of $40 per month, as well as an additional $1 for each arrest he made. He was the only salaried employee of the town of Fort Lauderdale and thus had a wide variety of other duties, including tax assessor, tax collector, and trash collector.

The department expanded to two officers in 1916. The first officer to receive the title of "Chief of Police" was appointed in 1920. Between 1924 and 1926, the FLPD increased in size from two officers to 26 officers, possibly due in part to an expanding real estate market. However, the state experienced a depression in 1926 and, by 1930, the FLPD had been reduced to only six officers. During this period, FLPD was rocked by scandal when, in 1925, federal prohibition officers arrested the Broward County sheriff and all deputy sheriffs as well as the FLPD chief and six officers for conspiracy to transport and sell alcohol.

The FLPD's web site[3] discusses the "hobo express," which the department ran during the depression. Essentially, FLPD officers were instructed to get 'undesirables" out of town. They would transport vagrants, homeless persons, and other unwanted individuals to the boundary between Fort Lauderdale and Deerfield Beach, a city directly to the north. Those individuals who refused transport were given a sentence of 30 days in jail.

In 1941, the establishment of civil service converted the department to a merit system of hiring, although during World War II there was a distinct shortage of qualified personnel. In the mid-1940s, the police reserves was formed, although the first volunteers had little training and their duties consisted of tasks such as helping with booking procedures and answering telephones in the department. In 1967, the department started a Police Youth Auxiliary and a Police Community Relations Unit. In 1974, uniformed policewomen were first put out on patrol. Two years later, the department instituted the first Community Service Aid program in the United States. This program, which was later converted to the present Police Safety Aide Program, trained civilians to handle accidents and to take police reports in non-violent incidents.

As of December, 2003, a total of twelve members of the FLPD have been killed in the line of duty, including eleven male officers of various ranks and one female civilian employee (a parking enforcement officer or "meter checker").[4]

Currently, the FLPD employs almost 500 sworn personnel and has an annual operating budget of almost $60 million. The department is accredited by the Commission for Florida Law Enforcement Accreditation. FLPD also operates the only municipal jail in Florida, opened in 1983. Some of the space is used for city prisoners awaiting trial or serving a misdemeanor sentence. In addition, in an effort to reduce costs, part of the space is leased to a number of federal agencies, including the Immigration and Naturalization Service, the Drug Enforcement Agency, the U.S. Border Patrol, the U.S. Marshals Service, and the Federal Bureau of Investigation.[5]

Currently, the minimum entrance requirements for the FLPD include:

- U.S. citizen
- be at least 19-years-old upon appointment
- have, or be eligible for, a valid Florida drivers license and have an acceptable driving record
- good moral character
- no felony convictions
- no misdemeanor convictions involving perjury or false statement
- no dishonorable discharge from the Armed forces
- high school graduate or the equivalent

Applicants who meet these requirements must go through a variety of tests, including a written examination, an oral interview, medical, psychological, and polygraph examinations, a background check, a physical agility test, and a swim text. Recruits then attend the police academy, studying a wide variety of subjects including Florida law and rules of evidence, the laws of arrest, search and seizure, patrol techniques, firearm techniques, defensive techniques, and first aid. After graduation, new probationary officers go through a field training program. Base salaries start at $40,393.60 while in the academy.[6]

The Orlando Police Department

According to the Orlando Police Department's web site[7], the city of Orlando was incorporated in 1875 and the first marshal was elected the same year. He was killed in the line of duty one year later, allegedly by an Orange County Deputy Sheriff. A deputy was added to the **Orlando Police Department** (OPD) in 1881, doubling the size of the department to two officers; a third officer was added in 1884. In 1892, officers began wearing black uniforms (they changed to brown in 1958).

By 1920, the department had increased to 32 officers, who received a salary of $900 per year. The department purchased its first police car that year and established a modern fingerprint identification system. OPD began its first formal training program for new officers in 1939. Prior to this program, new recruits were given a badge and gun and sent out on the streets. The new training program included instruction in criminal law, criminal investigation, the use of firearms, and basic life-saving techniques. The first two female police officers were hired in 1942, probably because of the reduction in the city's male population as a result of World War II. Although these officers were given patrol cars, their duties were very limited in scope; they were restricted to only those cases which involved women and children. The first black officers were hired in the 1950s.

The opening of Walt Disney World in 1971 significantly increased the workload of the OPD; the increase in tourism also led to an increase in the size of the department. In 1984, the OPD started the first Citizen's Police Academy in the United States. Many other police departments around the country have followed their lead and started similar programs; recently other public service agencies such as fire departments have begun citizen academies as well.

As of December, 2000, a total of twelve OPD officers have been killed in the line of duty. The most recent, Officer Tanya B. King, died on May 18, 2000 and was the first female officer to die on duty in Orange County, Florida.[8]

The OPD currently has a total of 669 sworn personnel.[9] The department was accredited by the Commission on Accreditation for Law Enforcement Agencies (CALEA) in 1997. Currently, the minimum entrance requirements for the OPD include:

- minimum age of 21
- U.S. citizen
- high school graduate or the equivalent, with some college-level coursework preferred
- have a valid drivers license for at least one year
- good physical condition
- vision correctable to 20/20
- good moral character
- no felony convictions
- no misdemeanor convictions that involve moral character or perjury
- resident within a 30-mile radius or 45-minute driving distance of Orlando Police Headquarters

OPD has stated that candidates with a college degree, military experience, police experience, and/or Florida Police Certification are much more likely to be considered by the department.[10]

Applicants who meet these requirements must go through a variety of tests, including a written civil service examination, a background check, medical, polygraph, psychological, and physical abilities examinations, and an oral interview. Recruits then attend the police academy, studying a wide variety of subjects including Florida law and rules of evidence, the laws of arrest, search and seizure, patrol techniques, firearm techniques, defensive techniques, and first aid. Academy graduates then go through a 19-week field training program. Base salaries start at $36,200 after the recruit graduates from the academy. The top officer base salary is currently $58,014. There are a variety of additional pay and bonus opportunities within the department.[11]

Orlando is one of the most popular tourist destinations in the United States today; this significantly affects the workload and duties of the OPD. As a response to the constant increase in tourism, the OPD established the **International Drive Team** in 1994 as a way of supplementing the existing patrol of this high-trafficked tourist area. International Drive (or "I-Drive") contains several theme parks (including the Universal Studios properties and the Wet-N-Wild water park) as well as a large number of hotels, motels, restaurants, and other tourist-related businesses and attractions. The I-Drive Team includes one sergeant, ten officers, and a civilian crime prevention practitioner.

Much of the patrol is done on police mountain bikes. The focus on crime prevention includes targeting both tourists and businesses, and providing a variety of materials and presentations.

COUNTY POLICING

Each of the 67 counties in Florida has a separate sheriff's department. According to the Florida Constitution, sheriffs serve terms of four years.[12] In most cases, the sheriff is elected by the county voters. However, the Constitution does allow for individual counties to select sheriffs by other means if they so desire.[13] For example, the sheriff of Miami-Dade County is appointed by the County Manager. The Constitution does not set forth any legal minimum requirements which must be met by candidates running for sheriff.

Sheriff's departments in Florida are full-service police agencies that provide police services to all unincorporated areas of the county. In addition, incorporated cities that do not wish to set up their own city police department may contract out to their county sheriff's department for police services. Chapter 30 of the Florida Statutes outlines the duties, responsibilities, appointment, etc., of sheriffs and deputy sheriffs in Florida. Sheriff's departments in Florida are often responsible not only for providing law enforcement services to the county, but also for running the county jail, maintaining security in all county courts, serving civil and criminal processes, and providing assistance when needed to local departments within the county. This assistance can range from operating a county-wide crime lab to assisting a local department with a criminal investigation.

The state of Florida has had county sheriffs since 1821, when Andrew Jackson, then serving as the state's military governor, passed an ordinance requiring the appointment of a sheriff to each court. Sheriffs and federal marshals shared the responsibility for enforcing the law until Florida became a state in 1845; at that time, the Florida State legislature enacted a law requiring the selection of a sheriff by the electors of each county. The term of office was two years; it was lengthened to the present four-year term in 1868. Sheriffs in Florida are responsible to the state governor for the enforcement and execution of all state criminal laws within their respective counties.

According to the Florida Department of Law Enforcement, as of June 2000, there were a total of 17,534 sworn law enforcement officers employed in county sheriff's offices in Florida. Of these, approximately 87 percent are male and 13 percent are female. Approximately 21 percent of all county deputies are non-white. The largest sheriff's office is the Miami-Dade Police Department with over 3,000 sworn officers, and the smallest is the Lafayette County Sheriff's Office, which has only three sworn officers.[14]

The Miami-Dade Police Department

The **Miami-Dade Police Department** (MDPD) is the largest police department in Florida and is responsible for providing police services to unincorporated Miami-Dade County. The county, which was originally known as Dade County, was established in 1836 and included what is now

Dade, Broward, Palm Beach, and Martin counties. The county seat was originally located in Juno and was moved to Miami in 1899. During the 19th century, county sheriffs were appointed by the state governor. From 1899 to 1966, the Dade County sheriff was an elected position.[15]

In 1957, the Dade County Sheriff's Office was renamed the Public Safety Department. Three years later, they were given the responsibility for providing police services to the Miami International Airport and the Port of Miami. They also had a variety of non-police-related responsibilities, including fire protection, animal control, motor vehicle inspection, and the operation of the county jail. However, by 1973, many of these responsibilities were removed so that the department could focus on policing and law enforcement.

In 1966, county voters decided that sheriffs in Dade County would no longer be elected but would be appointed by the County Manager. The official title of the Dade County sheriff is the "Director of the Public Safety Department and Sheriff of Metropolitan Dade County." In 1981, the Department received another name change; they were renamed the Metro-Dade Police Department. In 1997, after the name of the county was changed from "Dade County" to "Miami-Dade County," the Department was renamed the Miami-Dade Police Department. MDPD is accredited by CALEA.

In 2002, MDPD employed a total of 3,170 sworn officers.[16] The department is responsible for policing all unincorporated areas in the county. There are also a number of incorporated cities which contract with the department for their law enforcement services.

Currently, the minimum entry requirements necessary to be considered as an officer candidate include:

- minimum age of 19
- U.S. citizen
- high school graduate or the equivalent
- possess a valid driver's license
- vision not exceeding 20/100 uncorrected and correctable to at least 20/30
- normal color vision
- weight proportionate to height
- good physical condition
- no felony convictions
- no misdemeanor convictions that involve moral turpitude

Applicants who meet these requirements must go through a variety of tests, including a written civil service examination, a background check, medical and psychological screenings, a polygraph examination, a physical abilities test, and an oral interview. Recruits accepted as police officer trainees first attend the police academy and are then paired with a field training officer for supervised field training. Base salaries start at $32,514.[17]

The Broward County Sheriff's Office

Broward County, which is located directly north of Miami-Dade County, is served by the **Broward County Sheriff's Office** (BSO). BSO was founded in 1915 and is one of the largest sheriff's departments in the state. It provides law enforcement services for unincorporated Broward County as well as to a number of cities which contract with the department for protective services. It is also responsible for policing the Fort Lauderdale-Hollywood International Airport and Port Everglades and for the operation of the county jail system. In October, 2003, BSO became responsible for the administration of county fire rescue services. BSO is accredited by CALEA, and its correctional facilities have been accredited by the American Corrections Association (ACA) and the Florida Corrections Accreditation Commission. In 2003, BSO employed over 2,800 certified deputies.[18] Approximately half of these are sworn law enforcement officers while the rest are involved with the county corrections program.[19]

The agency is divided into three main divisions: the Department of Law Enforcement, the Department of Detention and Community Control, and the Department of Fire Rescue and Emergency Services. The **Department of Law Enforcement** provides police and law enforcement services to the county. It has 15 districts which include Port Everglades, the Fort Lauderdale-Hollywood International Airport, unincorporated Broward County, and a number of cities that have contracted with BSO to provide law enforcement services. The Department of Law Enforcement also operates a number of special divisions or units. The BSO Crime Lab provides technological services to all law enforcement agencies in the county as well as providing services to agencies throughout the state of Florida. School Resource Officers are assigned to county public schools to prevent juvenile delinquency and school crime and to develop and promote positive relationships between police and juveniles. The Strategic Investigations Division is devoted to organized crime and works closely with federal, state, and local law enforcement agencies. Other special units and divisions include the Aviation Unit, the Career Criminal Unit, the Civil Division, the Cold Case Unit, and the Marine Patrol.[20]

The **Department of Detention** operates the Broward County Jail system, which is the 13th largest local jail system in the United States. It has earned state accreditation from Florida's Corrections Accreditation Commission as well as national accreditation from the American Correctional Association's Commission on Accreditation for Corrections. BSO maintains four primary jail facilities, with an average daily population exceeding 5,000 inmates: the Main Jail, the North Broward Detention Center, the Joseph V. Conte Facility, and the Stockade Facility. A new women's facility located next to the Joseph V. Conte Facility is expected to open in 2004. Currently, approximately 77,000 inmates are booked into the BSO jail system each year.[21]

STATE POLICING

There are two main types of **state police agencies** within the United States. Some states, such as Pennsylvania, operate a **centralized** or full-service state police agency which includes both highway patrol functions and criminal investigation. However, other states, such as North Carolina, separate or **decentralize** the functions and keep criminal investigations separate from the uniformed highway patrol. Florida, which uses the decentralized model, has approximately three dozen state agencies with law enforcement powers. Main agencies include the Florida Department of Law Enforcement (FDLE) and the Florida Highway Patrol (FHP).

The Florida Highway Patrol

The **Florida Highway Patrol** (FHP) is a division of the state **Department of Highway Safety and Motor Vehicles**. The FHP was created in 1939 by an act of the Florida State Legislature. The first FHP training program was held in November of that year, with a class of 40 recruits, 32 of whom graduated to become patrolmen.

In 2001, the FHP had an authorized strength of 2,278 total personnel, including 1,777 sworn officers and 501 civilian (non-sworn) personnel. Approximately 30 percent of these are minority officers, including both racial/ethnic minorities and women. In addition, the department has 44 volunteer reserve officers, who have police authority, and 379 volunteer auxiliary members, who are authorized to carry firearms and to wear a uniform, but who are not authorized to make arrests. The FY 2001/2002 budget was approximately $161.7 million. A total of 37 members of the FHP have died in the line of duty.[22]

The primary mission of the FHP is to maintain safe highways. Other priorities include the prevention and deterrence of drunk driving, the apprehension of alcohol-impaired drivers, speed limit enforcement, and the promotion of seat-belt use. The department currently has a zero-tolerance policy with regard to the use of seat-belts and conducts regular "Safety Belt Blitzes" to increase compliance with the use of occupant restraints. During 2000, the FHP issued almost 82,000 citations for safety-belt violations. During the same year, over 294,000 speed-related arrests were made and over 114,000 warnings were issued.[23]

In addition, the FHP has a number of special activities. The Drug Interdiction Program focuses on the prevention and detection of drug trafficking in the state of Florida. The program has a total of 50 specially-trained troopers and 31 dogs who patrol both the interstate system and other major highways in Florida. The program also provides training to all sworn officers in drug identification and use detection. The department has 168 Traffic Homicide Investigators who investigate fatal traffic crashes. During FY 2001/2002, a total of 1,728 fatal traffic crashes were investigated by the FHP. Finally, the FHP's Bureau of Investigations includes 61 sworn officers as well as 11 non-sworn personnel. Troopers assigned to this detail investigate a variety of vehicle-related crimes, including auto theft, theft of drivers' licenses, odometer fraud, emissions fraud, title fraud, and highway violence.[24]

Currently, the minimum entrance requirements for the FHP include:

- minimum age of 19

- U.S. citizen
- a valid driver's license (not necessarily from the State of Florida)
- weight proportionate to height
- vision correctable to 20/30 in each eye
- a high school diploma or the equivalent as well as one of the following:
    - one year of law enforcement experience (sworn or non-sworn);
    - two years active, continuous, honorable military service;
    - two years of public contact experience; or
    - at least 30 semester-hours or 45 quarter-hours of college credit.

The FHP gives preference to applicants who have completed at least 60 semester- or 90 quarter-hours of college course work, or who have had at least two years of continuous military service (with an honorable discharge), or who have a current law enforcement certification from the State of Florida.

Applicants must pass a series of examinations, including written, physical, psychological, and polygraph examinations, as well as a background check and a physical aptitude test. FHP recruits go through a 26-week training program at the FHP's academy in Tallahassee and must pass the state certification exam. Recruits who are already certified by the state may go through an abbreviated 12-week transition academy. The recruit's first duty assignment is a ten-week field training program. The annual starting salary for state troopers in most counties is $31,596.00. Starting salaries are higher in certain counties, including West Palm Beach, Broward, Miami-Dade, Monroe, Collier, and Lee Counties.[25]

The Florida Department of Law Enforcement

The **Florida Department of Law Enforcement** (FDLE) was created by the Florida state legislature in 1967 as the Bureau of Law Enforcement. It was renamed the FDLE in 1969 after widespread government restructuring. The Executive Director of the FDLE is appointed by the state governor with the approval of at least three Cabinet members. The FDLE provides a variety of services to local, state, and federal law enforcement agencies in three primary areas: criminal justice investigation and forensic sciences; criminal justice information; and criminal justice professionalism.

The FDLE's **Criminal Justice Investigation and Forensic Sciences Services Program** provides both investigative and technical services to law enforcement agencies throughout the state. These services include gathering and sharing criminal intelligence, investigating public corruption, assisting in the location of missing children, apprehending criminals, and providing various protective services to the state governor and to visiting dignitaries. The FDLE operates twenty regional and field offices and seven crime laboratories which are located throughout the state and provide forensic expertise to law enforcement agencies. They also maintain the state's DNA database.

The FDLE's **Criminal Justice Information Program** maintains a variety of databases which are intended to provide information which may help law enforcement agencies prevent crime, recover stolen property, and identify and apprehend offenders. These databases contain information about wanted persons, missing persons, stolen property, parole status, domestic violence injunctions, and other issues which may be of use to law enforcement. Any Florida criminal justice agency can access these databases through the **Florida Crime Information Center** (FCIC II); they are also available to law enforcement agencies in other states through the **National Crime Information Center** (NCIC) network. The program also maintains the state's criminal history records and the **Automated Fingerprint Identification System** (AFIS), which currently contains almost 2 million fingerprint cards. The **Florida Statistical Analysis Center** analyzes statewide crime and criminal justice data and provides information to policymakers, planners, program developers, and to the public as a whole.

The **Criminal Justice Professionalism program** is responsible for maintaining a high level of police professionalism, training, and ethics throughout the state. The FDLE's **Criminal Justice Standards and Training Commission**, which is made up of 19 elected and appointed criminal justice officials, sets minimum training standards for police officers, offers the Officer Certification Examination, and offers a variety of advanced training programs for sworn officers. The Commission also investigates officers who fail to maintain these minimum standards and may revoke certification. The **Florida Criminal Justice Executive Institute** provides leadership training for the state's criminal justice executives.[26]

SPECIAL TYPES OF POLICE

Tribal Police

Florida contains several federally-recognized Indian Tribes which have tribal reservations in the state. There are two tribal police departments: the **Seminole Department of Law Enforcement** and the **Miccosukee Police Department**. Because some of the reservation land is held by the tribes under exclusive use permits granted by the U.S. Department of the Interior, tribal police in Florida have combined local, state, and federal law enforcement authority.

The Miccosukee Indians were originally part of the Lower Creek Tribes and lived in what is now Alabama and Georgia. They moved to the Florida panhandle in the early 1700s. However, after the Creek War and First Seminole War in the early 1880s they moved south to Alachua. In 1823, the Treaty of Moultrie Creek resulted in the tribe moving to a reservation in Central Florida. However, the adoption of the Indian Removal Act in the early 1830s led to the Second Seminole War (1835-1842) and later the Third Seminole War (1855-1858). To escape being deported to the western United States, members of the Miccosukee tribe hid in the Everglades. The present tribe is descended from a group of approximately fifty tribal members who successfully avoided deportation.

In 1976, the tribe established the **Miccosukee Police Department** (MPD) with federal funding from the Bureau of Indian Affairs. The Department patrols the tribal reservation, which is located in Miami-Dade and Broward Counties and borders three additional counties in the state of Florida. Some of the reservation is situated on Florida state land; other areas are on federal land.

Because of this, MPD officers have law enforcement authority from a variety of sources and have federal arrest powers. All MPD officers must first pass the Florida state certification examination and receive certification as a police officer in the state of Florida. Each officer is also commissioned as a Bureau of Indian Affairs Special Deputy Officer by the U.S. Department of the Interior and receives commissions by both the National Park Service and the U.S. Fish and Wildlife Service. This allows tribal police officers to handle all crimes under U.S. Title Code 18 as well as enforcing all Florida state statutes.[27]

The MPD is a full-service police department with 31 sworn officers.[28] It is one of the few tribal police departments in the United States which employs both Native Americans and non-Native Americans as police officers. The department provides all policing services that would be expected of any municipal police agency.

State University or Campus Police

The Florida State University System (SUS) is made up of ten public universities, each of which has a **campus police** force. All officers serving on a state university police force are certified by the state as law enforcement officers and have the same police authority as any other law enforcement officer in Florida. Officers have the authority to make arrests on any property owned or controlled by the State University System Board of Regents. The University of Florida is located in Gainesville, which is in the Florida panhandle. The **University of Florida Police Department** (UFPD) has 89 sworn officers who are responsible for providing police services to the university. The majority of these officers are assigned to the patrol division, and patrol the campus in patrol cars, on bicycles and motorcycles, and on foot. The UFPD has received both state and national accreditation and is the second-largest nationally accredited university police department in the United States. Officers enforce the law on SUS property, although they may also make arrests off campus when pursuit of the suspect originated on campus.[29]

The **Florida International University (FIU) Police Department** is the only other campus police department in Florida to receive both state and national accreditation. The FIU Police Department provides police services to multiple campuses , including patrol, criminal investigation, traffic enforcement and traffic investigation, crime prevention, and special events management. Officers are certified by the State of Florida.[30] The department has a total of 42 sworn officers. In addition, the Public Safety Aide Program uses students to provide additional campus security and to staff a campus escort service.[31]

School Police

Miami-Dade County Public School System has a **Division of School Police** (DSP) which provides law enforcement services to students, parents, teachers, and administrators. The DSP was organized in 1957 and is currently the fourth-largest public school system police department in the country. It is responsible for enforcing the law on all county school board properties. The division employs 184 sworn officers and 25 non-sworn support personnel who provide services to 331 schools throughout the county. A School Resource Officer is assigned to every middle school and senior high school in the county to develop crime prevention and intervention programs, student/parent conferences, counseling, and other necessary services. Three K-9 officers perform school searches and assist in raising safety awareness among students and school staff. DSP officers are state-certified law enforcement officers with full police powers. The division reports to the Miami-Dade County Superintendent of Schools.[32]

The DSP is involved in a wide variety of special law enforcement programs. The **Truancy Intervention Program** uses the Miami-Dade County Public School computer database to identify juveniles who are truant (have five or more un-excused absences). The student and his or her parents or guardians must attend a mandatory meeting at the school with a representative of the State Attorney's Office, DSP officers school attendance personnel, school counselors, and representatives from any necessary social services agencies. The **School Crime Hotline** is a confidential 24-hour telephone tip line which may be used by students wishing to anonymously report illegal activities in their school. The **Youth Crime Watch of Dade County** organizes youth crime watch clubs in county schools in an effort to create safer schools and reduce school crime. Other county-wide programs in which the DSP participates include the **Juvenile Assessment Center**, the **Multi-Agency Gang Task Force**, the **Serious Habitual Offender Comprehension Action Program**, **National Crime Prevention Month**, and **Project Clean Sweep**.[33]

POLICE TRAINING

Police departments today require highly-qualified and well-trained officers. In Florida, FS 943.11 authorized the creation of the **Criminal Justice Standards and Training Commission** (CJSTC) within the FDLE. The Commission membership is specified by section 1a of the statute and has a total of 19 members, including government officials, police officers, correctional officers, and civilians. Fifteen Commission members are appointed by the governor and serve four-year terms, although a term of appointment automatically ends if the member ceases to hold the office or employment which made him or her eligible for membership in the Commission. There is no compensation for service on the Commission.

The CJSTC is responsible for the design, evaluation, and implementation of training curricula for criminal justice officers (police and corrections), including not only recruit and in-service training but also advanced, specialized, and career development. The Commission develops and administers the state-wide certification examination for criminal justice officers and maintains employment, training, certification, and discipline records for certified officers in Florida. In addition, the CJSTC is responsible for administering sanctions when officers violate Commission standards or Florida Statutes.[34]

FS 943.13 outlines the minimum standards for employment or appointment as a law enforcement officer (including full-time, part-time, and auxiliary officers). These include the following:

- be at least 19 years old
- be a United States citizen
- be a high school graduate or equivalent (G.E.D.)
- no felony convictions
- no misdemeanor convictions involving perjury or false statements
- must have received an honorable discharge from the U.S. Armed Forces (if applicable)
- must pass a physical examination by a licensed physician
- must pass a background investigation proving good moral character
- must complete the basic recruit training program (unless exempt under the statute)
- pass the Florida Officer Certification Examination

These are state-mandated minimum requirements. However, FS 943.137(1) states that any law enforcement agency may establish "qualifications and standards for employment, appointment, training, or promotion of officers that exceed the minimum requirements..." For example, in 1997, the Commission's Physical Abilities Test (PAT) was approved as a recommended test and is now used by many of the state's criminal justice agencies, including the FHP. The PAT determines if applicants have the ability to perform various physical tasks which are required of criminal justice officers in Florida. The test includes eight tasks which must be completed within a specified time limit. The Commission currently recommends a time limit of six minutes and four seconds, although each agency may set its own time limit. The eight tasks include:

1. exiting vehicle, opening trunk, and removing several items (to measure eye-hand coordination, dexterity, and reaction time);
2. a 220-yard run (to measure muscular endurance);
3. an obstacle course (to measure muscular endurance, coordination, and flexibility);
4. a 150-pound dummy drag (to measure muscular endurance, flexibility, agility, and strength);
5. an obstacle course (repeat of task 3);
6. a 220-yard run (repeat of task 2);
7. a dry fire of a hand weapon with both dominant and non-dominant hand (to measure dexterity, muscular endurance, and strength); and
8. place items in trunk and enter vehicle.[35]

Other tests which may be required by local departments include:

- psychological examination
- oral examination
- written examination
- swim test
- drug test
- a minimum number of college credits

The CJSTC has developed basic recruit training programs to provide recruits with the skills required to become certified as Florida state criminal justice officers. Currently, there are 39 criminal justice training academies in the state which have been certified by the commission. Various Florida Statutes mandate specific training issues which must be covered in basic skills training. For example, FS 943.171(1) states that:

> Every basic skills course required in order for law enforcement officers to obtain initial certification shall ... include a minimum of 6 hours of training in handling domestic violence cases. Such training must include training in the recognition and determination of the primary aggressor in domestic violence cases.

Other statutory requirements for basic training include a minimum of eight hours training in interpersonal skills with diverse populations[36]; a minimum of four hours of training on victim rights and victim assistance[37]; instruction on HIV infection and AIDS[38]; instruction in the protection of archaeological sites and artifacts[39]; and instruction on the investigation of juvenile sexual offenders.[40]

Florida also requires all law enforcement officers to pass a statewide Officer Certification Examination. FS 943.17(e) requires the CJSTC "implement, administer, maintain, and revise a job-related officer certification examination..." for graduates of law enforcement, corrections, and correctional probation academies. According to FS 943.1397, no individual may be certified as an officer until he/she has passed the Officer Certification Examination with an acceptable score. The examination shows that the individual has the minimum knowledge needed to perform as a law enforcement officer in the state of Florida.

To be eligible to take the Officer Certification Exam, individuals must meet one of the following criteria:

- have completed a CJSTC-approved basic recruit training program within the past four years; or

- be an inactive, Florida-certified law enforcement officer with a break in service of over four years who has completed the required reinstatement training; or

- have received an exemption from completing the CJSTC-approved basic recruit training program and have completed the required equivalency training.[41]

The Law Enforcement Certification Examination includes the following subjects:

- legal
- interpersonal skills
- communications
- law enforcement investigations

- law enforcement patrol
- defensive tactics
- weapons
- vehicle operations
- law enforcement traffic
- medical first responder

Once certified, officers must complete a minimum of 40 hours of in-service training every four years to maintain their certification. This training must include eight hours of training relating to diverse populations[42] and training in juvenile sexual offender investigation.[43]

NOTES

1. Information obtained from the *2002 Criminal Justice Agency Profile*, available on the Florida Department of Law Enforcement home page (http://www.fdle.state.fl.us/cjst/CJAP/2002/)
2. *Ibid*
3. Fort Lauderdale Police Department home page (http://ci.ftlaud.fl.us/police)
4. *Ibid*
5. *Ibid*
6. *Ibid*
7. Orlando Police Department home page (http://www.cityoforlando.net/police/)
8. *Ibid*
9. *2002 Criminal Justice Agency Profile, op cit.*
10. Orlando Police Department home page, *op cit.*
11. *Ibid*
12. Florida State Constitution, Article VIII, Section 1d
13. *Ibid*
14. *2002 Criminal Justice Agency Profile, op cit.*
15. Miami-Dade Police Department home page (http://www.mdpd.com)
16. *2002 Criminal Justice Agency Profile, op cit.*
17. Miami-Dade Police Department home page, *op cit.*
18. Broward County Sheriff's Office home page (http://www.sheriff.org)
19. *2002 Criminal Justice Agency Profile, op cit.*
20. Broward County Sheriff's Office home page, *op cit.*
21. *Ibid*
22. Florida Highway Patrol home page (http://www.fhp.state.fl.us)
23. *Ibid*
24. *Ibid*
25. *Ibid*
26. Florida Department of Law Enforcement home page (http://www.fdle.state.fl.us)
27. Miccosukee Police Department home page (http://legal.firn.edu/tribal/miccosukee)
28. *2002 Criminal Justice Agency Profile, op cit.*

29. University of Florida Police Department home page (http://police.ufl.edu)
30. Florida International University Police Department home page (http://www.fiu.edu/%7Eunivpol/)
31. *2002 Criminal Justice Agency Profile, op cit.*
32. Miami-Dade Schools Police Department (http://police.dadeschools.net/)
33. *Ibid*
34. Criminal Justice Standards and Training Commission home page (http://www.fdle.state.fl.us/cjst/commission)
35. Florida Highway Patrol- Physical Abilities Test Instructions (http://www.fhp.state.fl.us/html/pat.html)
36. FS §943.1715
37. FS §943.172
38. FS §943.1725
39. FS §943.1728
40. FS §943.17291
41. Florida Administrative Code, Rule 11B-30.006
42. FS §943.1716
43. FS §943.17295

CHAPTER 5

THE COURT SYSTEM IN FLORIDA

The criminal court system in Florida is a two-tiered system, with two levels of appellate courts and two levels of trial courts. The two appellate courts in Florida are the Supreme Court of Florida and the District Courts of Appeal. The trial courts include state circuit courts and county courts.[1]

UNITED STATES DISTRICT COURTS

There are a number of federal courts which sit in Florida. These are not part of the Florida state court system and should not be confused with the state trial and appellate courts.

There are three **federal district courts** which sit in Florida. These are the trial courts of the federal system and include:

- the Northern District Court, which serves 23 counties
- the Middle District Court, which serves 35 counties
- the Southern District Court, which serves nine counties.[2]

The **U.S. Courts of Appeals** are the intermediate appellate court of the federal court system and have appellate jurisdiction only over federal laws. Judges in these courts serve life terms. They are nominated by the President of the United States and confirmed by the Senate. Florida, along with Alabama and Georgia, is part of the Eleventh Circuit. A total of twelve judgeships are allotted for this circuit.[3] The U.S. Court of Appeals should not be confused with the Florida District Courts of Appeal, which are part of the Florida state court system and are discussed below.

THE FLORIDA SUPREME COURT

The **Florida Supreme Court** is the highest court in the state and is the court of last resort in Florida. Its decisions are binding upon all other courts in the state. The first Florida State Constitution created the state Supreme Court but did not provide for any justices. The first Court's powers were vested in circuit court judges who were elected by the state legislature and served as Supreme Court justices from 1846 to 1851. Because there were four judicial circuits in Florida, there was a maximum of four circuit judges serving on the Supreme Court. In 1851, after a Constitutional amendment and the passage of several acts, the Supreme Court was given three justices who were elected by the legislature. In 1853, another constitutional amendment provided for the justices to be elected by the people and to serve six-year terms. The adoption of later constitutions, constitutional amendments, and legislative actions have frequently affected the method of selection of Supreme

Court justices as well as the length of their terms of office. Some of the changes that occurred over the years include:

- The 1861 constitution provided for Supreme Court justices to be appointed by the governor, with the advice and consent of the Senate, and to serve six-year terms.

- The 1868 constitution (adopted after the Civil War) provided for the Chief Justice and two associate justices to be appointed by the governor and confirmed by the Senate, and extended the term of office to a life term (or "during good behavior").

- The 1885 constitution provided for three justices to be elected by the people to six-year terms.

- A 1902 constitutional amendment increased the number of justices to six.

- A 1911 action by the state legislature reduced the Court's membership to five justices.

- A 1923 action by the state legislature increased the Court's membership to six justices.

- A 1940 constitutional amendment increased the Court's membership to the current seven justices.[4]

Seven justices sit on the Florida Supreme Court, including a Chief Justice and six associate justices. Five justices make up a quorum and at least four judges must agree for a binding decision to be reached.[5] Originally, Florida judges were elected by the voters. However, this system led to ethical conflicts when attorneys practicing before the Court donated money to judges' campaign funds. As a result, in the 1970s, Florida moved to a system of selecting and retaining judges based on merit, rather than by election. Currently, Supreme Court justices are appointed by the governor, who selects them from a list of three qualified possible appointees which is provided by the Judicial Nominating Commission. When a justice's six-year term of office expires, his or her name is placed on the next general election ballot for a "merit retention vote." The ballot asks the question, "Shall Justice _____ be retained in office?" If a majority of voters cast votes in favor of retaining the incumbent justice, he/she remains in office; if not, the governor appoints another individual to fill the vacancy in the Court.[6]

The Chief Justice of the Florida Supreme Court, who presides at all Court proceedings, is elected by a majority vote of the justices. The office rotates every two years. The Chief Justice is the chief administrative officer of Florida's entire judicial system. One of his or her duties is to swear in every newly-elected state governor.[7]

Article V, Section 8 of the Florida Constitution outlines the requirements necessary to be eligible to serve as a Supreme Court justice. These include:

- be a qualified elector of the state of Florida

- reside in the state of Florida

- be less than 70 years of age (no justice may serve after reaching age 70 except on a temporary basis or to complete less than one-half of a term of office)

- be a member of the Florida Bar for the preceding ten years

The Supreme Court sits in the Supreme Court Building in Tallahassee. It holds two terms each year; the first begins on January 1 and the second on July 1.[8] As the final court of appeals in the state, the Supreme Court has a variety of responsibilities, including both mandatory and discretionary reviews. These are outlined in the Florida State Constitution.[9] Mandatory review are those cases which the Court is required by law to hear. These include:

- final orders imposing a sentence of death

- any decisions by a district court which declare a state statute or provision of the state constitution to be invalid

- proceedings for the validation of bonds and certificates of indebtedness

- certain decisions of the state's Public Service Commission relating to utility rates and services (e.g., electric, gas, or telephone service)

In addition, the Court has the discretionary power to review certain decisions of the state district courts of appeal (although this review is not required). According to Article V, Section 3(b)(3), the Supreme Court:

> May review any decision of a district court of appeal that expressly declares valid a state statute, or that expressly construes a provision of the state or federal constitution, or that expressly affects a class of constitutional or state officers, or that expressly and directly conflicts with a decision of another district court of appeal or of the supreme court on the same question of law.

The Court also has the authority to issue certain extraordinary writs, which are orders requiring a person to perform a particular act or to refrain from performing a particular act. The Court may issue a variety of writs, including writs of prohibition, *mandamus*, *quo warranto*, and *habeas corpus*, as well as any other writs which are necessary to complete its responsibilities.[10]

The Court also has a variety of other judicial duties. It advises the state governor on issues which relate to the governor's constitutional duties and powers. It develops and circulates the rules which outline practice and procedure in all state courts; a two-thirds vote of the membership of the state legislature is required to repeal any rule. It is responsible for regulating the admission and discipline of lawyers in the state; to perform these duties, the Court created the Florida Bar and established the Florida Board of Bar Examiners as well as adopting a state-wide Judicial Code of Conduct. The Supreme Court is also responsible for disciplining judges and justices and, if necessary, removing them from office. They are assisted in this task by the Judicial Qualifications Commission, which investigates possible judicial misconduct and makes recommendations to the Court. Finally, one Supreme Court justice must be present in the Court whenever an execution is being carried out. The justice is part of a three-way telephone conversation between the Court, the state prison, and the governor's office. Although it has never happened, the justice does have the power to order the execution delayed.

FLORIDA DISTRICT COURTS OF APPEAL

Florida district courts of appeal are the state's intermediate appellate courts of review. The majority of trial court cases which are appealed do not reach the Florida Supreme Court but are reviewed by the state's district courts of appeals. These were established in 1957 by Article V of the Florida State Constitution. Prior to this time, all appeals were heard by the Supreme Court. However, the increasing problem of delay and congestion within the Supreme Court led to the development of the current two-tier appellate court system, with the district courts acting as a "buffer" between the lower trial courts and the State Supreme Court. By handling the majority of the appellate work in the state, district courts of appeal allow the Supreme Court to review only those cases that raise important legal questions and to ensure that decisions made throughout the state are uniform.[11] The district courts of appeals are discussed in Article V, Section 4 of the Florida State Constitution and Chapter 35 of the Florida State Statutes.

Currently, Florida is divided into five appellate court districts, with one district court of appeal serving each district.[12] The districts are headquartered in Miami, West Palm Beach, Lakeland, Daytona Beach, and Tallahassee.[13] There are over sixty district court judges in Florida.[14] The same rules that govern the selection of Supreme Court justices also apply to the selection of district court judges.[15] Judges serve six-year terms and may serve successive terms by undergoing a merit retention vote of the electors in their districts.[16] Cases are heard by panels of three judges and the agreement of two judges is necessary for a decision to be rendered.[17]

The district courts hear all appeals from the two trial courts except for those cases that are directly appealable to the Supreme Court (such as death penalty cases). Decisions are based on the merits of the case, using the record from the original trial court; the district courts do not hear additional testimony or retry the case. The court's primary purpose is to review the judgment made by the trial court to determine if a legal error was made. In most cases, the decision of the district court of appeals represents the final appellate review of a litigated case and is therefore final, although further appeals may be made to either the Florida Supreme Court or the U.S. Supreme Court. However, neither court is required to hear these appeals, and the vast majority of such requests for appeal are denied.

The district courts also have the authority to issue a variety of extraordinary writs, including writs of *certiorari*, prohibition, *quo warranto*, and *habeas corpus*, as well as any other writs which are necessary to complete its responsibilities.[18]

FLORIDA CIRCUIT COURTS

Florida has a two-tiered trial court system. The upper tier is made up of the **circuit courts** which are also known as **courts of general jurisdiction**, because they hear both civil and criminal cases. Each of the twenty judicial circuits in the state of Florida is served by a circuit court. The number of judges in a circuit varies, depending on the circuit's caseload and population, although each case is heard by only one judge. Currently, there are over 500 circuit court judges in the state.[19] The Eleventh Judicial Circuit, which serves Miami-Dade County, is the largest of the 20 circuits in the state, with 71 circuit court judges and 41 county court judges. This Circuit alone hears approximately 800,000 cases per year, including civil traffic infractions.[20]

According to the Florida State Constitution, the requirements necessary to be eligible for the office of circuit court judge include being a resident of the state of Florida, a qualified elector of the state, and a member in good standing of the Florida bar for the preceding five years.[21] Circuit court judges are elected by the voters of their respective judicial circuits and serve terms of six years. The judges of each circuit select a chief judge who is responsible for all administrative responsibilities for all trial courts within the circuit, including both circuit and county courts.

Circuit courts have original jurisdiction over all cases of law which are not assigned by state statute to the county courts. This includes all criminal felony prosecutions, all juvenile cases (except traffic offenses), any civil disputes that involve more than $15,000, and a variety of other matters. Circuit courts also have appellate jurisdiction over most cases that originated in the county courts. When serving as an appellate court, circuit court judges may issue extraordinary writs of *certiorari*, prohibition, *mandamus*, *quo warranto*, and *habeas corpus*.[22]

FLORIDA COUNTY COURTS

Article V, Section 6 of the Florida State Constitution mandates that there be a **county court** in each of the 67 counties in Florida, with at least one judge for each court. The number of judges in each county court varies, depending on the county's population and caseload, and is specified in FS §34.022. In most counties, the requirements to be a county judge include being a county resident and a member of the Florida Bar for the past five years. However, in those counties with a population of 40,000 or less, the only requirement is to be a member in good standing of the Florida Bar. County judges are elected by the voters of the county and serve terms of four years.[24]

According to FS 34.01, county courts have original jurisdiction over all misdemeanor criminal cases, all violations of municipal and county ordinances, all landlord-tenant disputes, and all other civil disputes which involve no more than $15,000.

The County Court of the Eleventh Judicial District has 41 county court judges, more than any other county court. It is divided into three divisions. The **County Criminal Division** handles misdemeanor criminal cases (except those handled by the Domestic Violence Division), all criminal traffic cases, violations of municipal and county ordinances, and many civil traffic infractions. The **County Civil Division** hears civil cases involving damages up to $15,000. The **Domestic Violence Division** is responsible for all criminal domestic-violence related misdemeanors, all cases involving violations of court-ordered injunctions, and cases involving violations of civil orders of protection.[24]

COURT ADMINISTRATION

The Florida Bar

The Florida Bar is an integrated or unified bar; all attorneys licensed to practice law in Florida must be active members of the Florida Bar, which is the state-wide professional organization of lawyers. It has been an integrated bar association since a Supreme Court ruling of 1949, which was made under its authority to regulate the practice of law in the state. The Florida Bar is the third largest mandatory state bar in the country, with over 73,000 members and over 300 employees in December, 2003. The headquarters of the Florida Bar is located in Tallahassee, with branch offices in Tallahassee, Tampa, Orlando, Ft. Lauderdale, and Miami.[25]

The Florida Bar unofficially originated in 1889 and consisted of a small voluntary group of lawyers. The Florida State Bar Association was organized in 1907. It remained a voluntary organization and helped develop legislative reform affecting the Florida court system and the legal profession in the state. The suggestion that Florida move to a unified bar was first proposed in the 1930s but the proposal was rejected by the Supreme Court. In 1947, the concept of compulsory membership was proposed again and in 1949 the Supreme Court accepted the idea. The name of the organization was shortened to "The Florida Bar," and all lawyers in the state were automatically made members in 1950.[26]

The Florida Bar assists the Supreme Court by making recommendations of disciplinary actions in grievance proceedings against attorneys, as well as in cases which involve complaints about the practice of law by unauthorized individuals. The Bar has 64 standing committees as well as a number of special committees. The Bar's governing body is known as the Board of Governors. Most of the 52 members are elected by the members of the Bar, although there are two public members who are not lawyers and who are appointed by the state Supreme Court.[27]

The Florida Board of Bar Examiners

The **Florida Board of Bar Examiners** was created by the Florida Supreme Court in 1955. It is an administrative agency of the judicial system and is responsible for making certain that only qualified individuals are admitted to the practice of law in the state. The Board has a total of 15 members. Twelve are practicing attorneys who have been members of the Florida Bar for at least five years. They are appointed by the Court from a list of three recommended appointees provided by the Board of Governors of the Florida Bar and serve terms of five years. The other three members of the Board are non-lawyers who have an academic four-year college degree and who serve three-year terms. They are appointed by the Court from a list of three recommended appointees provided by a joint committee made up of three members of the Board of Governors of the Bar and three members of the Board of Bar Examiners.[28]

The Board has a variety of functions which revolve around the process through which individuals who want to be admitted to the state bar demonstrate their eligibility. These include screening applicants on character and fitness as well as administering the Florida Bar Examination to determine applicants' professional competence. Final appointment to the Florida Bar is done by the state Supreme Court, not the Board of Bar Examiners.[29]

The Office of the State Courts Administrator

The **Office of the State Courts Administrator** was created in 1973 for the purpose of developing a standardized uniform system of case reporting which would provide information on judiciary activities. This information is used to prepare the annual operating budget and to predict future needs of judges and specialized court divisions. The State Courts Administrator is appointed by the Supreme Court and serves at the pleasure of the Court.

The State Courts Administrator is the liaison between the Florida court system and various other state government offices, including the executive branch, the legislative branch, the Court's auxiliary agencies, and various national court research and planning agencies. S/he supervises the administrative office of the Florida courts and represents the court system before the state legislature on any matters dealing with or affecting the court system.[30]

The Clerk and the Marshal of the Florida Supreme Court

Article V, section 3(c) of the Florida Constitution states that:

> The supreme court shall appoint a clerk and a marshal who shall hold office during the pleasure of the court and perform such duties as the court directs. Their compensation shall be fixed by general law.

The **clerk** maintains custody of the Court's papers, records, and files, as well as the Court seal. S/he is responsible for receiving all documents filed in cases, circulating this material to the

Supreme Court justices, and releasing opinions of the Court to the public. The clerk also maintains custody of the seal of the Supreme Court.

The **marshal** executes Court processes throughout Florida and has the power to deputize any county sheriff or deputy sheriff to assist in these duties. The marshal is also the custodian of the Supreme Court building and grounds and supervises Court security.[31]

FLORIDA CRIMINAL COURT PROCEDURES

The basic procedures involved in a criminal trial, including the pretrial activities, are similar in most states. In Florida, the criminal justice process begins when the police are notified (or in some other way discover) that a crime has been committed and they initiate an investigation into that crime. The procedures discussed in this section apply specifically to felony offenses; however, the procedures for misdemeanors are extremely similar.

Arrest and Booking

After the police have determined both that a crime has in fact been committed and that a specific person committed the crime, they may place that individual under **arrest**. In some situations, the police may have obtained an **arrest warrant** from a judge. FS 901.02 defines those situations in which a warrant of arrest may be issued. However, in Florida, as in most states, the vast majority of arrests are made by police officers acting without a warrant. The situations in which it is lawful to make an arrest without a warrant are outlined in FS 901.15.

Before being brought before a judge, the arrested suspect is taken to the county jail to undergo the **booking** procedure. This involves entering into the police record various facts about the suspect. The suspect will be photographed and fingerprinted and may be placed in a police lineup.

First Appearance

According to Rule 3.130(a) of the Florida Rules of Criminal Procedure (Fla.R.Cr.P.),

> Except when previously released in a lawful manner, every arrested person shall be
> taken before a judicial officer, either in person or by electronic audiovisual device in
> the discretion of the court, within 24 hours of arrest.

At the **first appearance**, the judge provides the defendant with several important pieces of information, including the nature of the charge against him or her. The defendant is also given a copy of the complaint. The judge is also required by Fla.R.Cr.P. 3.130(b) to advise defendants of their constitutional rights, including the right to remain silent, the right to counsel, and the right to communicate with counsel, family, or friends. At this time, if the defendant is indigent and cannot afford to hire an attorney, the court will appoint counsel.

The judge will also decide at this time whether the defendant is entitled to any form of **pretrial release**, including **bail**. Although the U.S. Supreme Court stated in *Stack v. Boyle*[32] that the U.S. Constitution does not guarantee the right to bail, the Florida State Constitution and the Florida Rules of Criminal Procedure do provide a substantive right to bail in many cases. According to Fla.R.Cr.P. 3.131(a),

> Unless charged with a capital offense or an offense punishable by life imprisonment and the proof of guilt is evident or the presumption is great, every person charged with a crime or violation of municipal or county ordinance shall be entitled to pretrial release on reasonable conditions. If no conditions of release can reasonably protect the community from risk of physical harm to persons, assure the presence of the accused at trial, or assure the integrity of the judicial process, the accused may be detained.

The court has a number of options when setting conditions of pretrial release. These include:

- payment of cash bail in exchange for pretrial release;

- payment of non-cash bail (usually a property bond where the defendant deposits some form of property as collateral for release);

- release on personal recognizance (where the defendant is released without any bail); and

- conditional release (where the defendant is required as a condition of pretrial release to attend a treatment or other program).

Pretrial Probable Cause Hearings and Adversary Preliminary Hearings

A defendant who is not granted pretrial release at the first appearance is entitled to a **nonadversary probable cause hearing** within 48 hours of arrest, although this time period may be extended for no more than 48 additional hours in certain situations.[33] This proceeding is only mandatory if the defendant was arrested without a warrant. If an arrest warrant was issued, then the determination of probable cause was made by a magistrate prior to the arrest and does not need to be made again.

If the defendant has been released from custody prior to the determination of probable cause, s/he may make a written motion for a nonadversary probable cause hearing if the specific conditions of the pretrial release place a significant amount of restraint on his or her liberty and if a finding of no probable cause would eliminate those conditions. The defendant has 21 days from the date of arrest to file a motion. The court then has seven days from the filing of the motion to make a probable cause determination.[34]

Effectively, during a nonadversary probable cause hearing, the judge is making the same determination after the arrest that would have been engaged in prior to the arrest if an arrest warrant had been applied for. If the judge finds that there is probable cause, the defendant is then held to answer to the charges. However, if the judge finds no probable cause, or if the time periods specified in the Florida Rules of Criminal Procedure are not followed strictly, the defendant must be released from custody unless s/he has been formally charged by the prosecution. If the prosecution has filed an information or indictment, "the defendant shall be released on recognizance subject to the condition that he or she appear at all court proceedings..."[35]

If the defendant is not charged by indictment or information within 21 days of arrest, s/he has the right to an **adversary preliminary hearing** on any felony charges that are pending. This procedure is conducted according to the same rules that apply at a criminal trial, including the examination and cross-examination of witnesses, including the defendant. During the preliminary hearing, the prosecutor presents evidence intended to show that there is probable cause to believe both that a crime was committed and that the defendant committed it. If the magistrate determines that there is probable cause to believe that an offense has been committed, and that the defendant has committed it, the defendant will be "held to answer" to the charges in circuit court. If the magistrate finds that there is no probable cause, the defendant will be released from custody unless the prosecutor has filed formal charges in the form of an information or indictment. In that situation, the defendant is released on his or her own recognizance. The procedures governing the adversary preliminary hearing are discussed in Fla.R.Cr.P. 3.133(b).

Indictment, Information, and the Grand Jury

According to Article I, Section 15 of the Florida State Constitution,

> No person shall be tried for capital crime without presentment or indictment by a grand jury, or for other felony without such presentment or indictment or an information under oath filed by the prosecuting officer of the court, except persons on active duty in the militia when tried by courts martial.

The Florida Rules of Criminal Procedure also hold that anyone charged with an offense punishable by death must be prosecuted by **a grand jury indictment** while individuals charged with any other felony may be prosecuted either by indictment or by **information.**[36] In practice, nearly all non-capital felony crimes are charged by information.

Chapter 905 of the Florida Statutes outlines the procedures relating to the grand jury. The purpose of the grand jury is to determine whether or not there is sufficient evidence to justify a formal indictment against an accused individual. If the grand jury decides that the evidence constitutes probable cause to believe that a crime has been committed by the accused, a **true bill of indictment** is issued and the defendant may then be tried. In Florida, the grand jury is composed of 15 to 21 individuals.[37] For a true bill to be issued, a minimum of 12 jurors must vote to return an indictment.[38] If the grand jury finds that there is insufficient evidence to show that the accused individual committed the crime, a **no bill** will be issued and the case dismissed.

According to FS 905.24,

> Grand jury proceedings are secret, and a grand juror ... shall not disclose the nature
> or substance of the deliberations or vote of the grand jury.

No member of the grand jury may state or testify in any court how members of the grand jury voted or what opinions were expressed during deliberation. While a record of the proceedings is maintained, it is confidential. Witnesses who appear before the grand jury have no constitutional right to counsel, although they do receive the Fifth Amendment protection against self incrimination.

In a capital case, after a true bill has been issued by the grand jury, the prosecution enters a formal indictment before the court. In non-capital cases, the prosecution may enter an information before the court if the magistrate at the preliminary hearing rules that there is sufficient evidence to formally charge the defendant. FS 923.03 provides examples of the proper forms of indictment and information. The defendant is entitled to receive a copy of the indictment or information at least 24 hours before s/he is required to plead to the charges.[39]

Arraignment and Plea

The next stage in the criminal process is the **arraignment**. During the arraignment, the charging document is read aloud to the defendant in open court. At this point, the defendant also enters a **plea**. Because this stage is essentially a formality, a defendant who is represented by counsel is allowed to have his or her attorney file a written plea of not guilty at or before the arraignment and thus waive the actual arraignment.[40]

In most cases, defendants will plead either guilty or not guilty. However, with the consent of the court, a defendant may plead *nolo contendere*, which indicates that, although the defendant is not admitting guilt, s/he does not contest the charges. A judge will not always permit a plea of *nolo contendere*. If a defendant stands mute or refuses to plead, a plea of not guilty is entered into the record.[41] If the defendant has been charged with a misdemeanor, s/he may have been given the opportunity to plead at the first appearance; if s/he plead guilty, the judge may have entered judgment and sentence at that time without requiring additional formal charges to be filed. If a defendant enters a plea of guilty or *nolo contendere* to a felony, s/he waives the right to a trial and proceeds directly to the sentencing phase of the criminal court procedures.

Plea Bargaining

While plea bargaining is not a formal stage of the criminal justice process, it is an extremely important process in every state, including Florida. The majority of all felony and misdemeanor convictions in Florida are the result of guilty pleas. Generally, plea bargaining involves an attempt to resolve or dispose of a case without a trial. According to Fla.R.Cr.P. 3.171(a),

> Ultimate responsibility for sentence determination rests with the trial judge.
> However, the prosecuting attorney and the defense attorney, or the defendant when

representing himself or herself, are encouraged to discuss and to agree on pleas that may be entered by a defendant. The discussion and agreement must be conducted with the defendant's counsel. If the defendant represents himself or herself, all discussions between the defendant and the prosecuting attorney shall be of record.

During this process, the prosecutor negotiates with the defense attorney (or the defendant). In most cases, the purpose or goal of the negotiation is to reach an agreement whereby the defendant will enter a plea of guilty (or *nolo contendere*) to a charge. This may be the original charge or a lesser or related charge. In exchange for this plea, the prosecutor may do one or more of the following:

- drop other charges which have been filed against the defendant;

- make recommendations to the court concerning sentencing;

- agree not to oppose the defendant's request for a certain sentence; or

- agree to a specific sentence.

The defense attorney is responsible for advising the defendant of all plea offers and any other relevant matters that may affect the defendant's decision, such as the possible results of each plea. The defense attorney may not accept any plea bargain without the full consent of the defendant. The trial judge does not participate directly in plea bargaining. However, the judge is still an important element in the process because all plea bargains must be approved by the judge. Plea bargaining often begins at the preliminary hearing stage but may continue up to and even during the trial.

Discovery

After the charging document has been filed, the defense has the opportunity to engage in the **discovery process**, by obtaining additional information about the prosecution's case and inspecting any physical evidence possessed by the prosecutor. The discovery process is outlined in detail in Fla.R.Cr.P. 3.220. In addition, the Florida "Sunshine Law," states that "It is the policy of this state that all state, county, and municipal records shall be open for personal inspection by any person."[42] Under this statute, defense counsel may request access to a wide variety of public records.

To participate in discovery, the defendant files a "Notice of Discovery" with the court; this document is also served on the prosecution. Once this is done, the prosecution has 15 days to provide the defense with the following information:

- names and addresses of all individuals known to the prosecution who have information that may be relevant to the crime or to the defense

- any statements made by any of these individuals

- any statements made by the defendant and the name(s) of any witnesses to these statements

- any statements made by any co-defendants

- the portions of recorded grand jury minutes that contain the defendant's testimony

- any papers or objects obtained from the defendant or that belong to the defendant

- whether the prosecution has any information or material provided by a confidential informant

- whether there was any electronic surveillance used against the defendant

- whether there was any search or seizure and any documents relating to the search or seizure

- any reports or statements of experts

- any tangible papers or objects which were not obtained from or belonged to the defendant but which the prosecution intends to use at a hearing or at trial [43]

Florida's discovery process is reciprocal. This means that not only does the prosecution provide the defendant with information, but the defense may also be required to provide certain information to the prosecution. According to Fla.R.Cr.P. 3.220(d)(1), within 15 days of receiving the list of names and addresses from the prosecutor, the defense must provide the prosecution with a list (names and addresses) of all witnesses the defense expects to call as witnesses at a hearing or at trial. In addition, the defense must disclose to the prosecution any statements made by defense witnesses (other than the defendant), any reports or statements made by experts, and any papers or objects the defendant intends to use in the hearing or trial.

Pre-Trial Motions

There are a number of **pre-trial motions** that may be filed in Florida criminal court. A **motion to dismiss** is filed by the defense and claims that the charges against the defendant should be dropped because:

- the defendant has already been pardoned for the offense being charged

- the defendant has previously been placed in jeopardy for the offense being charged

- the defendant has previously been granted immunity for the offense being charged

- the facts do not establish a clear case of guilt against the defendant.[44]

A **motion to continue** (or **motion for continuance**) may be filed by either the defense or the prosecution and requests that the case be delayed for a specific period of time.[45] A **motion to suppress evidence** considers whether evidence was obtained through an unlawful search and seizure and should therefore be prohibited from use as evidence in court. According to Fla.R.Cr.P. 3.190(h)(1), the grounds for suppressing evidence include:

(A) the property was illegally seized without a warrant;
(B) the warrant is insufficient on its face;
(C) the property seized is not that described on the warrant;
(D) there was no probable cause for believing the existence of the grounds on which the warrant was issued; or
(E) the warrant was illegally executed.

This motion generally applies to physical evidence. To suppress testimonial evidence, the defendant must file a **motion to suppress a confession or admission** which claims that the defendant's confession or admission was obtained illegally.[46] Finally, a **motion for a change of venue** may be filed by either the prosecution or the defendant. This motion requests that the location of the trial be changed on the grounds that it is not possible to obtain a fair and impartial trial in the county where the case is currently pending.[47]

The Right to a Speedy Trial

The Florida State Constitution provides for the right to a speedy trial.[48] In Florida, each case must be brought to trial within a certain specified period of time.[49] In general, if the defendant is charged with a misdemeanor by indictment or information, s/he must be brought to trial within 90 days. If the crime with which the defendant is charged is a felony, s/he must be brought to trial within 175 days. However, if the defendant is responsible for delays in bringing the case to trial, these delay periods are not included in the maximum pre-trial period. If the defendant has not been brought to trial within the prescribed period of time, s/he may file a notice with the court of expiration of speedy trial time. No more than five days from the filing of this notice, the court must hold a hearing on the notice and, unless there is a legitimate reason for the delay as outlined in Fla.R.Cr.P. 3.191(j), must order the defendant be brought to trial within ten days. If the defendant is not brought to trial within this period, and s/he is not responsible for the delay, the judge, upon a defense motion, must dismiss the case.

Trial

The vast majority of all criminal cases are disposed of by a plea of guilty on the part of the defendant. If the defendant enters a plea of not guilty and the case does go to **trial**, the procedure is similar regardless of whether the case involves a felony or a misdemeanor.

According to both the Sixth Amendment to the U.S. Constitution and Article I, Section 16 of the Florida State Constitution, all defendants have the right to a speedy, public, and impartial trial. The Florida State Constitution also guarantees the right to a **jury trial**. However, with the court's approval, a defendant may waive his or her right to a jury trial.[50] In these cases, the defendant will be given a **bench trial**. A bench trial is held before a judge and there is no jury present.

In Florida, criminal cases are tried before a six-member jury. For capital cases, a twelve-person jury is used.[51] Although some states now require only a majority vote of guilty, Florida still requires a unanimous vote of all jury members before a defendant may be declared guilty.

Jury Selection

The first step in a jury trial is the **selection of the jury**. The **venire**, or list of possible jurors, is compiled annually by the Department of Highway Safety and Motor Vehicles (DMV). Individuals who meet the following criteria are qualified to serve as jurors in Florida:

- 18 years of age or older;

- a U.S. citizen;

- a legal resident of Florida and the county in which they are called to serve;

- possess a driver's license or identification card from the DMV[52]

FS 40.013 mandates that the following individuals be excluded from jury service in Florida:

- any individual who is being prosecuted for or who has been convicted of a felony, unless s/he has been restored to civil rights;

- the governor, lieutenant governor, all members of the state cabinet, clerks of court, and judges;

- all full-time federal, state, county, or local law enforcement officers (although they may choose to serve); and

- anyone who has an interest in the issue that is to be tried.

The statute also states that the following individuals may be excused from jury service upon request:

- expectant mothers;

- any parent who is not employed full time and who has custody of a child under six years of age;

- anyone who was summoned and who reported as a prospective juror within the past year;

- anyone 70 years of age or older; and

- anyone who is responsible for the care of a person who is unable to care for himself or herself because of any physical or mental incapacity.

The trial judge also has the option of excusing any practicing attorney, any practicing physician, any individual who is physically infirm, or anyone else for reasons of hardship, extreme inconvenience, or public necessity. In addition, FS 913.13, states that individuals whose beliefs would prevent them from finding a defendant guilty of a capital crime shall not be qualified as a juror in a case involving a crime punishable by death.

The process of jury selection is known as **voir dire** and involves an examination of the prospective jurors by the court and by the attorneys for both the prosecution and the defense. The stated purpose of the *voir dire* is to determine whether each potential juror is impartial and will be able to render a fair verdict in a case. Potential jurors are placed under oath and then questioned by the judge, prosecutor, and defense counsel.

During the process, both the defense and the district attorneys are allowed to make challenges, or to object to the inclusion of certain potential trial jurors. Florida allows two types of challenges. **Challenges for cause** generally are based on the attorney's belief that the juror is biased in some way that will prevent him or her from acting impartially and without prejudice during the trial. FS 913.03 outlines the specific grounds on which a challenge for cause may be made:

> A challenge for cause to an individual juror may be made only on the following grounds:
> (1)   The juror does not have the qualifications required by law;
> (2)   The juror is of unsound mind or has a bodily defect that renders him or her incapable of performing the duties of a juror, except that, in a civil action, deafness or hearing impairment shall not be the sole basis of a challenge for cause of an individual juror;
> (3)   The juror has conscientious beliefs that would preclude him or her from finding the defendant guilty;

(4)   The juror served on the grand jury that found the indictment or on a coroner's jury that inquired into the death of a person whose death is the subject of the indictment or information;

(5)   The juror served on a jury formerly sworn to try the defendant for the same offense;

(6)   The juror served on a jury that tried another person for the offense charged in the indictment, information, or affidavit;

(7)   The juror served as a juror in a civil action brought against the defendant for the act charged as an offense;

(8)   The juror is an adverse party to the defendant in a civil action, or has complained against or been accused by the defendant in a criminal prosecution;

(9)   The juror is related by blood or marriage within the third degree to the defendant, the attorneys of either party, the person alleged to be injured by the offense charged, or the person on whose complaint the prosecution was instituted;

(10)   The juror has a state of mind regarding the defendant, the case, the person alleged to have been injured by the offense charged, or the person on whose complaint the prosecution was instituted that will prevent the juror from acting with impartiality, but the formation of an opinion or impression regarding the guilt or innocence of the defendant shall not be a sufficient ground for challenge to a juror if he or she declares and the court determines that he or she can render an impartial verdict according to the evidence;

(11)   The juror was a witness for the state or the defendant at the preliminary hearing or before the grand jury or is to be a witness for either party at the trial;

(12)   The juror is a surety on defendant's bail bond in the case.

Peremptory challenges may be used by either attorney to remove potential jurors from the jury panel without giving any specific reasons. According to FS 913.08, if the offense for which the defendant is charged is punishable by death or life imprisonment, the defense and the state each are entitled to ten peremptory challenges. For all other felony offenses, the defense and state each are entitled to six peremptory challenges. For all misdemeanors, the defense and state may have up to three peremptory challenges.

After the selection of the jury is completed, the jurors are sworn in by the court. Fla.R.Cr.P. 3.360 specifies the oath of trial jurors:

> The following oath shall be administered to the jurors: "Do you solemnly swear (or affirm) that you will well and truly try the issues between the State of Florida and the defendant and render a true verdict according to the law and the evidence, so help you God?" If any juror affirms, the clause "so help you God" shall be omitted.

Opening Statements

Both the prosecutor and the defense attorney are entitled to make an opening statement which provides all the participants in the trial, especially the jury, with an overview of the facts of the case. In Florida, the prosecutor makes the first statement. After the prosecution's opening remarks are completed, the defense may make an opening statement or may choose to wait until the start of the defense case.

Presentation of the Prosecution's Evidence

After the opening statements are completed, the prosecution begins to present evidence in support of the charge that has been brought against the defendant. The prosecution presents first because the state is bringing the charge against the defendant and, because of the presumption of innocence, has assumed the burden of proof. Evidence submitted into court may include documents, pictures, recordings, depositions, objects, pictures, or witness testimony. The judge determines the admissibility of each piece of evidence, based on the rules set forth in the Florida Evidence Code.[53] These rules are intended to ensure that unreliable evidence, or evidence that was illegally obtained, is not accepted into court.

The prosecutor generally begins with **direct examination** of the prosecution's first witness, who is obviously expected to give evidence to support the state's case against the defendant. After the prosecutor finishes questioning the witness, the defense is allowed to **cross-examine** the same witness. If the prosecutor wishes, s/he may then return to ask the witness more questions in a process known as **re-direct examination**. Following this, the defense attorney has the option to question the witness once more during the **re-cross examination**. This procedure is repeated for each witness called by the prosecution.

Presentation of the Defense's Evidence

After the prosecution has presented all its evidence and called all its witnesses, the defense may then offer evidence. If the defense attorney chose not to make an opening statement at the start of the trial, s/he may make one now. The defense then proceeds to present its evidence. The procedure for the presentation of the evidence by the defense is similar to that of the prosecution: direct examination, cross examination, re-direct, and re-cross. The defendant is not required to testify at any point in the trial; both the U.S. Constitution and the Florida State Constitution protect the defendant against self-incrimination.

Rebuttal and Surrebuttal

After the defense has presented its evidence, the prosecution is entitled to present a **rebuttal** case. At this time, the prosecutor may present evidence in response to the case presented by the defense. The defense may also be entitled to present a **surrebuttal** case, which involves presenting evidence after the prosecution has completed the rebuttal. However, this is at the discretion of the trial court.

Closing Arguments

Once all the evidence is presented, each side is given the opportunity to make a **closing argument** which is addressed directly to the jury. During this stage of the trial, each attorney reviews and summarizes the evidence that best supports his/her side of case, discusses any inferences that may be drawn from that evidence, and points out weaknesses in the opponent's case. In Florida, the prosecution makes its closing arguments first, followed by the defense.

Instructions to the Jury

After the closing arguments are completed, the judge has the opportunity to provide instructions to the jury regarding any legal issues or points of law which are applicable to the case. This step is also known as **charging the jury**. The judge may not sum up the evidence or make comments on the credibility of witnesses or the guilt of the defendant. Only in a capital case may the judge instruct the jury as to the possible sentence that may be imposed for the offense for which the defendant is being tried. The Florida Bar publishes *Florida Standard Jury Instructions* which contains a set of standard instructions used by judges in Florida to instruct the jury regarding legal issues.

Jury Deliberation and Verdict Rendition

After the judge has given instructions to the jury, the jury retires to the jury room for **deliberation**. At this time, the jurors discuss the case and attempt to come to agreement on a verdict concerning the guilt or innocence of the defendant. Florida law requires that all jurors agree on a guilty verdict before the defendant can be convicted of the charge. If the jurors are unable to agree on a verdict after a reasonable period of time, they are **deadlocked** and considered to be a "**hung jury**." If this happens, the judge will declare a **mistrial** and the case may have to be retried in front of a new jury.

If the jurors come to an agreement on a **verdict**, they are returned to the courtroom by the bailiff and the verdict is read in open court. After the verdict is rendered, the jurors must be collectively asked whether this is their verdict. In addition, either the defense or the prosecution is entitled to request a poll of the individual members of the jury to ensure that each member of the jury agrees with the verdict and that no member was coerced or intimidated into agreeing, or agreed simply out of exhaustion. If in either the collective or individual poll, any juror responds negatively, the court must refuse to accept the verdict and direct the jury to resume deliberations.

If the verdict of the jury is not guilty, the trial is over and the defendant must be immediately discharged from custody and is entitled to the return of any bail money and the exoneration of any sureties. The trial court judge is required to accept a verdict of not guilty. Because of the state and federal constitutional protections against double jeopardy, the defendant may never be tried in state court for those same charges.

Proceedings Between the Verdict and the Sentence

If the defendant is found guilty, s/he will be sentenced. However, after a verdict of guilty is rendered and before the sentencing phase of the trial, the defendant may make a **post-trial motion** to set aside or modify the verdict. If the judge sets aside the verdict, the defendant may be entitled to a dismissal, a reduction of the charges, or a new trial. These motions are rarely granted. However, if a new trial is granted, the defendant may not be prosecuted for an offense that is more serious than that of which s/he was originally convicted. For example, if in the original trial the defendant was charged with second degree murder, s/he cannot be charged with first degree murder in the new trial.[54]

The Sentence

If the defendant is found guilty, s/he will be sentenced by a judge. In most cases, the trial judge will pronounce the **sentence**, although in some situations it may be necessary for sentence to be pronounced by a different judge.

Chapter 921 of the Florida Statutes contains mandatory sentencing guidelines which must be followed by the judge when passing sentence. The maximum possible sentence depends on the level of the offense: for an infraction, the maximum sentence is a fine; for a misdemeanor, the maximum sentence is up to one year in a county jail; and for a felony, it is incarceration for at least one year in a state prison or, for murder with aggravating circumstances, death. Some counties also offer diversion programs that allow the judge to order the defendant to receive counseling, get medical treatment, or perform some type of community service work. The sentencing process is discussed in more detail in Chapter 6.

Appeal

If the defendant is convicted of a crime, s/he may have the option of **appealing** the conviction. The defendant has the right to appeal regardless of the crime of which s/he was convicted, the sentence received, or the type of trial.

An appeal does not involve retrying a case or even re-examining the factual issues surrounding the crime. It only involves an examination or review of the legal issues involved in the case. The purpose of an appeal is to make certain that the defendant received a fair trial and that s/he was not deprived of any constitutional rights at any time. In most cases, if a defendant wins on appeal, s/he will be retried.

NOTES

1.   Florida Supreme Court Historical Society (2002). *Handbook for Supreme Court Docents*. (http://www.flcourts.org/pubinfo/documents/HandbookDocents2002.pdf)
2.   See 28 U.S.C. 89
3.   See 28 U.S.C. 41
4.   Florida's Court System (http://www.flcourts.org/pubinfo/system2.html)
5.   Florida State Constitution, Article V, §3a
6.   Florida's Court System *op cit.*
7.   *Ibid*

8. FS §25.051
9. Florida State Constitution, Article V, §3b
10. Florida's Court System, *op cit.*
11. *Ibid*
12. FS §35.01
13. FS §35.05
14. FS §35.06
15. Florida State Constitution, Article V, §8
16. Florida's Court System, *op cit.*
17. FS §35.13 and Florida State Constitution, Article V, §4a
18. Florida's Court System, *op cit.*
19. Florida Statutes, Chapter 26
20. About the Eleventh Judicial Circuit of Florida
    (http://www.jud11.flcourts.org/about_the_court/)
21. Florida State Constitution, Article V, §8
22. Florida's Court System, *op cit.*
23. *Ibid*
24. About the Eleventh Judicial Circuit of Florida, *op cit.*
25. The Florida Bar home page (http://www.flabar.org/)
26. *Ibid*
27. *Ibid*
28. Rules of the Supreme Court Relating to Admission to the Bar
29. Florida Board of Bar Examiners (http://www.floridabarexam.org/)
30. Florida's Court System, *op cit.*
31. *Ibid*
32. *Stack v. Boyle*, 342 U.S. 1 (1951)
33. Fla.R.Cr.P. 3.133(a)(1)
34. Fla.R.Cr.P. 3.133(a)(2)
35. Fla.R.Cr.P. 3.133(a)(4)
36. Fla.R.Cr.P. 3.140(a)
37. FS 905.01
38. FS 905.23
39. Fla.R.Cr.P. 3.140(m)
40. Fla.R.Cr.P. 3.160(a)
41. Fla.R. Cr.P. 3.170©)
42. FS 119.01(1)
43. Fla.R.Cr.P. 3.220(b)(1)
44. Fla.R.Cr.P. 3.190©)(4)
45. Fla.R.Cr.P. 3.190(g)
46. Fla.R.Cr.P. 3.190(I)
47. Fla.R.Cr.P. 3.240
48. Florida State Constitution, Article I, §16
49. Fla.R.Cr.P. 3.191

50.   Fla.R.Cr.P. 3.260
51.   FS §913.10
52.   FS §40.01
53.   See Chapter 90 of the Florida Statutes
54.   Fla.R.Cr.P. 3.640(a)

CHAPTER 6

SENTENCING IN FLORIDA

INTRODUCTION

After a criminal defendant pleads guilty or is found guilty in court by a judge or jury, the judge must impose punishment upon the offender. Rule 3.700(a) of the Florida Rules of Criminal Procedure (Fla.R.Cr.P.) defines a **sentence** as "the pronouncement by the court of the penalty imposed on a defendant for the offense of which the defendant has been adjudged guilty." Sentences and other final case dispositions must be pronounced in open court and entered into the court minutes, or docketed if the court does not keep minutes.[1] Although sentencing may have a variety of purposes, FS 921.002(1)(b) states that, in Florida,

> The primary purpose of sentencing is to punish the offender. Rehabilitation is a desired goal of the criminal justice system but is subordinate to the goal of punishment.

Thus, it is clear that, in Florida, the sentencing judge is to focus on punishment rather than rehabilitation or any other goal. If sentencing goals conflict, the punishment of the offender always has the highest priority.

In every case in which a conviction has been entered, the court is required to pronounce sentence. If the defendant has been found guilty on multiple counts, the court must pronounce sentence on each count. In all cases, the judge determines the final sentence, although in those cases where the defendant has been convicted of a capital crime, the jury provides the sentencing judge with a recommendation as to the sentence to be imposed.

TYPES OF SENTENCES

A variety of sentences may be imposed upon convicted offenders in Florida. Sentences acceptable in the Florida courts include:

- fines
- restitution
- probation
- other community-based or intermediate sanctions (e.g., boot camp, house arrest with electronic monitoring, shock incarceration)
- incarceration in a jail or prison
- death

Combinations of these sentences are also allowed. For example, a judge may order both imprisonment and a fine, or order an offender to pay both a fine and victim restitution. However, the judge has only a limited amount of discretion when imposing a sentence because s/he must follow the sentencing guidelines set out in the Florida Statutes.

WHEN SENTENCING OCCURS

If a defendant enters a plea of guilty at the arraignment, there is no trial and the court proceeds directly to the sentencing phase. Defendants who plead guilty to a misdemeanor charge may be sentenced at the first appearance, unless the judge chooses to postpone sentencing and order the probation department to prepare a pre-sentencing report. If the defendant pleads guilty or *nolo contendere* to a felony charge at the arraignment, s/he waives the right to a trial and proceeds to the sentencing phase of the criminal court procedures.

If the defendant enters a plea of not guilty and is then found guilty in a criminal trial, the sentence may be imposed by the court immediately following the trial or in a sentencing hearing scheduled for a later date. If the crime for which the offender has been found guilty is a misdemeanor, the offender may be sentenced immediately following the jury's presentation of the verdict. However, if the jury reaches a guilty verdict in a felony case, the judge may order the probation department to prepare a pre-sentencing report and schedule a hearing. This report contains information about the offender's background and about the circumstances of the crime.

FLORIDA SENTENCING GUIDELINES

A Recent History of Sentencing in Florida

Until 1983, sentencing in Florida was primarily **indeterminate**. While the statutes provided for maximum penalties of incarceration for felonies based on the seriousness or degree of the felony, this still allowed judges a significant amount of discretion in the final sentencing decision. In addition, most offenders were eligible for parole. This created concerns about lack of uniformity in sentencing as well as disparities between time sentenced and time served, which eventually led to the development of sentencing guidelines for use when sentencing convicted felony offenders, and to the abolition of parole for most crimes. **Sentencing guidelines** establish mandatory minimum and maximum sentences for specific crimes, which judges are required to follow.

Florida first adopted sentencing guidelines in 1983. The **1983 Florida Sentencing Guidelines** currently apply to all non-capital felony offenses committed on or after October 1, 1983 and before January 1, 1994, and abolished parole eligibility for most offenses committed during this period. The 1983 guidelines included nine worksheets, each for a different offense category. Each worksheet allowed the determination of a point score for the offender being sentenced, based on the current offense, prior offenses, victim injury, etc. The total score determined the final sentence, although judges were allowed to depart from the guidelines if they provided a written statement outlining their reasons for such departures.

The 1983 guidelines assumed the concept of **truth in sentencing**, which means that it was expected that offenders would actually serve the amount of time to which they were sentenced. However, by 1989, the average percentage of sentence time actually served was 34 percent. This was due to a variety of factors, including lack of funding and increased population growth in the state.[2] As a result, the 1994 *Safe Streets Initiative* included a new set of sentencing guidelines. The **1994 Sentencing Guidelines** are currently in effect for all non-capital felonies committed between January 1, 1994 and September 30, 1995. They were "designed to emphasize incarceration in the state prison system for violent offenders and nonviolent offenders who have repeatedly committed criminal offenses and have demonstrated an inability to comply with less restrictive penalties previously imposed."[3]

The 1994 guidelines differ significantly from the 1983 guidelines. Instead of 9 separate worksheets, non-capital felonies are ranked by seriousness into one of ten offense severity levels, with one being the least and ten being the most serious. Offenders are assigned points based on the current offense, any additional crimes, and any prior record, as well as other factors such as victim injury, violations of supervision requirements, etc. The final sanction is based on the offender's total score.

The **Crime Control Act of 1995** significantly amended the 1994 guidelines, although it retained the basic structure. The result was to increase the severity of sanctions in many situations. Originally, the 1995 guidelines applied to all crimes committed between October 1, 1995 and September 30, 1998. However, in the 2000 case of *Heggs v. State*[4], the Florida Supreme Court found the 1995 sentencing guidelines to be in violation of the Florida State Constitution. In some cases, offenders would have received less severe punishments if sentenced under the 1994 guidelines than under the 1995 guidelines. The Court's ruling in *Heggs* affected offenders who committed crimes between October 1, 1995 and May 24, 1997. As a result, certain offenders were eligible to petition for re-sentencing under the 1994 guidelines. The 1995 sentencing guidelines still apply to offenders who committed crimes between May 25, 1997 and September 30, 1998.

In 1998, the state adopted the **Florida Criminal Punishment Code**, which superceded the earlier sentencing guidelines. This code applies to non-capital felonies committed on or after October 1, 1998; crimes committed prior to that date are sentenced under the appropriate earlier version of the guidelines. The discussion in this chapter will relate primarily to the Criminal Punishment Code, which is outlined in FS 921.002 et. seq., as opposed to the earlier sentencing guidelines which are outlined in FS 921.001 et. seq. However, offenders are sentenced under the guidelines or code that was in effect at the time the conviction offense was actually committed.

The Criminal Punishment Code allows increased judicial discretion in increasing sentence severity (essentially increasing upward discretion), allows for increased penalties for many crimes, and reduces the point threshold for mandatory prison time. Under the guidelines, the threshold for a mandatory sentence of incarceration was 52 points. However, under the Criminal Punishment

Code, offenders must score no more than 44 points to receive a sanction other than incarceration in a state prison facility.

Prior to the adoption of sentencing guidelines in Florida, almost all offenders who were sentenced to prison were eligible for parole. However, the various guidelines, and the Criminal Punishment Code, have abolished parole for most crimes. According to the Florida Parole Commission, individuals eligible for parole include:

> All persons sentenced prior to October 1, 1983, or convicted of crimes committed prior to October 1, 1983, and not sentenced under Sentencing Guidelines, who receive a sentence, or cumulative sentence, of 12 months or more (with the exception of persons sentenced to death), or those persons convicted of crimes who were sentenced with a 25 year minimum mandatory with eligibility for parole after service of the mandatory portion of the sentence and who have satisfactory prison conduct.[5]

Essentially, only those inmates who were sentenced prior to the passage of the 1983 sentencing guidelines, as well as some inmates who were convicted of non-capital felonies prior to October 1, 1995, are eligible for parole in Florida. No offender who committed a crime after October 1, 1995 is eligible for parole.

The Purpose of Sentencing Guidelines

One of the primary reasons for the creation of sentencing guidelines in Florida was to attempt to reduce sentencing disparity. FS 921.001(4) outlines the purpose of sentencing guidelines in Florida:

> The purpose of the sentencing guidelines is to establish a uniform set of standards to guide the sentencing judge in the sentence decisionmaking process. The guidelines represent a synthesis of current sentencing theory, historical sentencing practices, and a rational approach to managing correctional resources. The sentencing guidelines are intended to eliminate unwarranted variation in the sentencing process by reducing the subjectivity in interpreting specific offense-related and offender-related criteria and in defining the relative importance of those criteria in the sentencing decision.

Although the various versions of the sentencing guidelines only apply to offenders convicted of crimes committed before October 1, 1998, the Criminal Punishment Code has similar goals. According to FS 921.002(1), the Criminal Punishment Code reflects a series of key principles, including:

(a) Sentencing is neutral with respect to race, gender, and social and economic status.

(b) The primary purpose of sentencing is to punish the offender. Rehabilitation is a desired goal of the criminal justice system but is subordinate to the goal of punishment.

(c) The penalty imposed is commensurate with the severity of the primary offense and the circumstances surrounding the primary offense.

(d) The severity of the sentence increases with the length and nature of the offender's prior record.

(e) The sentence imposed by the sentencing judge reflects the length of actual time to be served, shortened only by the application of incentive and meritorious gain-time as provided by law, and may not be shortened if the defendant would consequently serve less than 85 percent of his or her term of imprisonment...

(f) Departures below the lowest permissible sentence established by the code must be articulated in writing by the trial court judge and made only when circumstances or factors reasonably justify the mitigation of the sentence. The level of proof necessary to establish facts that support a departure from the lowest permissible sentence is a preponderance of the evidence.

(g) The trial court judge may impose a sentence up to and including the statutory maximum for any offense, including an offense that is before the court due to a violation of probation or community control.

(h) A sentence may be appealed on the basis that it departs from the Criminal Punishment Code only if the sentence is below the lowest permissible sentence...

(i) Use of incarcerative sanctions is prioritized toward offenders convicted of serious offenses and certain offenders who have long prior records, in order to maximize the finite capacities of state and local correctional facilities.

In most cases, the sentencing pronounced by the sentencing judge must fall within the guidelines set out in the Florida Statutes. FS 921.00265(1) states that:

A departure sentence is prohibited unless there are mitigating circumstances or factors present ... which reasonably justify the departure.

A departure sentence is one which falls below the lowest permissible sentence as defined by the Criminal Punishment Code. In general, if the judge does go outside the recommendations of the Code, s/he must put the reasons in writing. In addition, in most cases, if the judge does impose a departure sentence, the defendant and the state have a right to appeal the sentence.

Factors Considered in Sentencing

When a judge is sentencing an offender for a specific criminal offense, s/he uses a special worksheet which allows the judge to create a score for that offense and offender. There are four main factors which are considered when scoring an offense. These are outlined in the **Florida Criminal Punishment Code Worksheet**[6] and include:

- the primary offense at conviction
- any additional offenses at conviction
- injury to the victim
- the offender's prior record

There are a variety of other factors that are included in the worksheet which may be considered by the sentencing judge.

The first factor in the guidelines worksheet is the **primary offense at conviction**. The primary offense is defined as:

> the offense at conviction pending before the court for sentencing for which to total sentence points recommend a sanction that is as severe as, or more severe than, the sanction recommended for any other offense committed by the offender and pending before the court at sentencing. Only one count of one offense before the court for sentencing shall be classified as the primary offense.[7]

Therefore, if the offender has committed multiple offenses, or multiple counts of the same offense, the primary offense for sentencing purposes is the one that will result in the most severe sanction. The other offenses are scored as additional offenses at conviction.

The second factor in the worksheet includes any **additional offenses at conviction**. Additional offenses are defined by FS 921.0021(1) as:

> ...any offense other than the primary offense for which an offender is convicted and which is pending before the court for sentencing at the time of the primary offense.

The third factor is that of **victim injury**. This is defined in FS 921.0021(7)(a) as:

> ...the physical injury or death suffered by a person as a direct result of the primary offense, or any additional offense, for which an offender is convicted and which is pending before the court for sentencing at the time of the primary offense.

Obviously, victim injury can only apply if the offender was convicted of a primary or additional offense which involved physical contact or impact with the victim (e.g., homicide, manslaughter, battery, robbery). In addition, there must be some actual physical injury or trauma to the victim. If, for example, the victim was slapped by the offender and no physical trauma resulted from the slap, no victim injury has occurred. Pregnancy and childbirth that result from a sexual battery do constitute physical trauma.

The offender's **prior record**, if any, is another factor used in the worksheet. This includes only those offenses of which the offender was actually convicted and that were committed prior to the crime for which the offender is being sentenced, regardless of whether the offender was an adult or juvenile at the time. The prior record may also include past convictions that occurred in other states, in federal or military courts, or in foreign countries, as well as violations of county or municipal ordinances. However, if an offender has had no convictions for at least ten years from the most recent date of release from confinement, supervision, or sanction, the offender's prior record is not scored. If the offender has a juvenile record, any prior juvenile dispositions which would have been considered criminal offenses if committed by an adult are not included if the time period between the date of disposition of the juvenile offense and the date of the commission of the primary offense is at least five years.[8]

Offense Severity Levels

When ranking the primary and additional offenses on the sentencing scoresheet, the offenses are ranked according to severity. There are ten offense levels, ranking from the least severe (1) through the most severe (10). In addition, the additional offense category includes a ranking of "M" which applies to misdemeanor offenses. FS 921.0022(3) provides an *Offense Severity Ranking Chart* which lists felonies by level of severity. If an offense is not listed specifically in the statute, then it is ranked as follows:

- third degree felonies are ranked as offense level 1
- second degree felonies are ranked as offense level 4
- first degree felonies are ranked as offense level 7
- first degree felonies punishable by life are ranked as offense level 9
- life felonies are ranked as offense level 10[9]

Scoring the Five Factors

FS 921.0024 provides a worksheet which shows exactly how offense scores are determined. For the primary offense, each level is associated with a specific number of points. For example, a Level 1 primary offense receives 4 sentence points, a Level 4 primary offense receives 22 points, and a Level 10 primary offense receives 116 points. Similarly, the additional offenses are associated with specific numbers of points, which must then be multiplied by the number of counts. For example, a Level 1 additional offense receives 0.7 points per count, a Level 4 additional offense receives 3.6 points per count, and a Level 10 additional offense receives 58 points per count. Misdemeanor additional offenses receive 0.2 sentence points per count.

There are seven levels of victim injury, each with a specific point count attached. These must be multiplied by the number of injuries. The least severe level is "slight", for which the offender receives 4 points per injury. The most serious level is "2nd degree murder-death" which receives 240 sentence points. Other levels include "sexual contact" and "sexual penetration." The number of primary offense points, additional offense points, and victim injury points are combined into a "Total Offense Score."

The prior record of the offender is scored in a manner similar to that used for the primary and additional offenses. If the offender's prior record includes misdemeanor offenses, s/he receives 0.2 points per count. If the prior record includes Level 1 offenses, the offender receives 0.5 points per count. Level 4 prior offenses are scored at 2.4 points per count, and Level 10 prior offenses are scored at 29 points per count. The total number of points attributed to the offender's prior record make up the "Total Prior Record Score."

There are a number of other factors which may also be considered, and which may result in additional points being added to the offender's score. These points, combined with the total offense score and total prior record score, make up the subtotal sentence points. The offender's **legal status** refers to the offender's status if s/he:

    (a) Escapes from incarceration;
    (b) Flees to avoid prosecution;
    (c) Fails to appear for a criminal proceeding;
    (d) Violates any condition of a supersedeas bond;
    (e) Is incarcerated
    (f) Is under any form of a pretrial intervention or diversion program; or
    (g) Is under any form of court-imposed or postprison release community supervision.[10]

If the offender was under no type of legal restriction at the time s/he committed the offense, no points are added to the scoresheet. However, if any form of legal status existed at the time the primary offense was committed, four sentence points are assessed. **Community sanction violations** include violations of probation, community control, or pretrial intervention or diversion.[11] If such a violation is before the court at the time of sentencing, six sentence points will be assessed per violation. If the offender has any primary or additional offenses ranked as Level 8, 9, or 10 and has committed any prior serious felonies (Level 8, 9, or 10) an additional thirty **prior serious felony** points will be added to the offender's score. **Prior capital felony points** are assessed if the offender has been found guilty in the past of a capital felony. In this case, the offender will receive additional sentence points equal to twice the number of points received for the primary offense and any additional offense. Finally, additional sentence points are added if the offender was in **possession of a firearm or semiautomatic weapon** while committing the felony for which s/he has been convicted.

The worksheet also includes a number of factors which are known as **sentencing multipliers**. Rather than having additional points added to the subtotal, the subtotal sentence points are multiplied by a given amount if one of these factors is present. The sentencing multiplier factors which may be considered include:

- **Drug trafficking** – if the offender's primary offense is level 7 or 8 drug trafficking, the subtotal sentence points may be multiplied by 1.5, at the court's discretion.

- **Law enforcement protection** – the subtotal sentence points are multiplied by a factor of 1.5, 2.0, or 2.5 if the primary offense is a violation of the Law Enforcement Protection Act.[12] The multiplier used depends on which provision of the Act the offender actually violated.

- **Grand theft of a motor vehicle** – if the primary offense is third degree grand theft of a motor vehicle and the offender has at least three prior convictions for the same offense, the subtotal sentence points are multiplied by 1.5.

- **Criminal street gang offense** – if the primary offense was committed for the benefit of a criminal street gang, the subtotal sentence points are multiplied by 1.5.

- **Domestic violence in the presence of a child** – if the primary offense of which the offender has been convicted is domestic violence, and the crime was committed in the presence of a child under the age of 16 who is a member of the family household, the subtotal sentence points are multiplied by 1.5.

After the sentencing multipliers are computed, they are combined with the subtotal sentence points to provide the total sentence points, which are then used to determine the recommended sentence.

Converting the Sentencing Points into a Recommended Sentence

After the sentencing worksheet has been completed and the total number of sentencing points assigned to the offender has been determined, the court uses this information to sentence the offender. FS 921.0024(2) outlines the recommended sentences:

- If the offender has no more than 44 total sentence points, the court may impose a sentence of incarceration in a local facility rather than a state prison.

- If the offender has more than 44 total sentence points, the lowest permissible sentence is incarceration. The number of months of the lowest allowable sentence is determined by first subtracting 28 from the total number of sentence points and then decreasing this number by 25 percent. For the sentence to be served in a state prison, it must exceed one year.

The calculation provides only the lowest allowable sentence; the permitted range is this lowest sentence up to and including the statutory maximum. FS 775.082 defines the statutory maximum sentence allowed for each category of offense, as follows:

(1) A person who has been convicted of a capital felony shall be punished by death if the proceeding held to determine sentence ... results in findings by the court that such person shall be punished by death, otherwise such person shall be punished by life imprisonment and shall be ineligible for parole.

(2) In the event the death penalty in a capital felony is held to be unconstitutional by the Florida Supreme Court or the United States Supreme Court, the court having jurisdiction over a person previously sentenced to death for a capital felony shall cause such person to be brought before the court, and the court

shall sentence such person to life imprisonment as provided in subsection (1). No sentence of death shall be reduced as a result of a determination that a method of execution is held to be unconstitutional under the State Constitution or the Constitution of the United States.

(3) A person who has been convicted of any other designated felony may be punished as follows:

    (a)

        1. For a life felony committed prior to October 1, 1983, by a term of imprisonment for life or for a term of years not less than 30.

        2. For a life felony committed on or after October 1, 1983, by a term of imprisonment for life or by a term of imprisonment not exceeding 40 years.

        3. For a life felony committed on or after July 1, 1995, by a term of imprisonment for life or by imprisonment for a term of years not exceeding life imprisonment.

    (b) For a felony of the first degree, by a term of imprisonment not exceeding 30 years or, when specifically provided by statute, by imprisonment for a term of years not exceeding life imprisonment.

    (c) For a felony of the second degree, by a term of imprisonment not exceeding 15 years.

    (d) For a felony of the third degree, by a term of imprisonment not exceeding 5 years.

(4) A person who has been convicted of a designated misdemeanor may be sentenced as follows:

    (a) For a misdemeanor of the first degree, by a definite term of imprisonment not exceeding 1 year;

    (b) For a misdemeanor of the second degree, by a definite term of imprisonment not exceeding 60 days.

(5) Any person who has been convicted of a noncriminal violation may not be sentenced to a term of imprisonment nor to any other punishment more severe than a fine, forfeiture, or other civil penalty...

Departing from the Criminal Punishment Code

The sentencing judge is expected to follow the guidelines recommended by the Criminal Punishment Code. However, there are some situations in which a sentencing judge is allowed to depart to some extent from the sentence recommended by the Code. FS 921.002(3) states that:

> A court may impose a departure below the lowest permissible sentence based upon circumstances or factors that reasonably justify the mitigation of the sentence ... The level of proof necessary to establish facts supporting the mitigation of a sentence is a preponderance of the evidence ... Any sentence imposed below the lowest permissible sentence must be explained in writing by the trial court judge.

Although the earlier sentencing guidelines outlined both aggravating and mitigating circumstances which allowed the sentencing judge to depart to some extent from the specific sentence outlined in the guidelines, the Criminal Punishment Code only provides for the existence of mitigating circumstances. **Aggravating circumstances** are factors about the crime or the offender which increase the seriousness of the crime or make it worse than usual in some way, whereas **mitigating circumstances** make a crime less serious in some way. FS 921.0026(2) lists a set of mitigating circumstances which may justify a departure from the lowest permissible sentence, including:

(a) The departure results from a legitimate, uncoerced plea bargain.

(b) The defendant was an accomplice to the offense and was a relatively minor participant in the criminal conduct.

(c) The capacity of the defendant to appreciate the criminal nature of the conduct or to conform that conduct to the requirements of law was substantially impaired.

(d) The defendant requires specialized treatment for a mental disorder that is unrelated to substance abuse or addiction or for a physical disability, and the defendant is amenable to treatment.

(e) The need for payment of restitution to the victim outweighs the need for a prison sentence.

(f) The victim was an initiator, willing participant, aggressor, or provoker of the incident.

(g) The defendant acted under extreme duress or under the domination of another person.

(h) Before the identity of the defendant was determined, the victim was substantially compensated.

(i) The defendant cooperated with the state to resolve the current offense or any other offense.

(j) The offense was committed in an unsophisticated manner and was an isolated incident for which the defendant has shown remorse.

(k) At the time of the offense the defendant was too young to appreciate the consequences of the offense.

(l) The defendant is to be sentenced as a youthful offender.

The statute specifically states that the defendant's state of intoxication at the time of the crime, or his/her addiction to intoxicating substances, is not a mitigating factor under the law and may not be used to justify a reduction in the sentence.[13]

The Criminal Punishment Code and Capital Offenses

According to FS 921.002, the Criminal Punishment Code does not apply to capital felonies. Instead, capital offenders are sentenced under conventional law. Offenders convicted of capital crimes have a bifurcated trial, in which the determination of guilt is separated from the sentencing phase. Whenever possible, trial and the sentencing proceeding are held before the same jury. At the sentencing hearing, the jury hears evidence and provides the court with an advisory sentence as to whether the offender should be sentenced to death or to life imprisonment. The court, regardless of the jury's recommendation, must consider the existence of aggravating and mitigating circumstances and may only impose a sentence of death if aggravating circumstances exist which are not outweighed by existing mitigating circumstances. A judgment of conviction and sentence of death are automatically appealed to the Florida Supreme Court.[14]

The topic of capital punishment is discussed in more detail in Chapter 7.

Concurrent versus Consecutive Sentences

According to FS 775.021(4)(a), if an offender commits several separate criminal offenses in the course of one criminal transaction, s/he shall be sentenced separately for each offense. There has been considerable debate in the courts regarding when multiple offenses are actually separate crimes. The statute states that

> ...offenses are separate if each offense requires proof of an element that the other does not, without regard to the accusatory pleading or the proof adduced at trial.

FS 775.021(4)(b) goes on to state that offenses are considered to be separate except in the following situations:

1. Offenses which require identical elements of proof.
2. Offenses which are degrees of the same offense as provided by statute.
3. Offenses which are lesser offenses the statutory elements of which are subsumed by the greater offense.

Essentially, offenses are considered to be separate when each of the offenses that was committed requires proof of a fact or element that is not required by the other offense. For example, the courts have held that the robbery of a husband and the murder of a wife are separate and distinct crimes and the offender may be convicted and sentenced for each. On the other hand, the courts have held that murder and attempted robbery with a firearm are not separate offenses but rather constitute one crime, so that only one conviction and one sentence are allowed.

If the offender is convicted of multiple separate criminal offenses, the court must impose a sentence for each offense. If the sentences imposed involve terms of imprisonment, the sentencing judge has the option of requiring the sentences to be served either concurrently or consecutively. **Concurrent sentences** are served at the same time, so that they overlap. **Consecutive sentences**, on the other hand, are served in succession, one after the other. For example, if an offender is convicted of two offenses and receives a sentence of four years imprisonment for each count, to be served concurrently, both sentences are satisfied after a total of four years. If, however, the sentences are to be served consecutively, the offender must serve a total of eight years to satisfy both sentences.

According to FS §921.16(1), if an offender is convicted of multiple offenses which were charged in the same indictment, information, or affidavit, s/he shall serve all sentences of imprisonment concurrently unless the court specifically directs that two or more of the sentences should be served consecutively. However, if an offender receives sentences of imprisonment for offenses that were not charged in the same indictment, information, or affidavit, the sentences shall

98

be served consecutively unless the court specifically directs that two or more of the sentences shall be served concurrently.

In other words, if an offender is charged with, and convicted of, multiple offenses (for example, multiple counts of armed robbery), the sentences imposed by the court shall be served concurrently. If, on the other hand, an offender was charged and convicted separately of multiple crimes, the sentences shall be served consecutively.

THE "10-20-LIFE" LAW

In 1998, guns were involved in over 31,000 violent felonies, including almost 14,000 armed robberies.[15] However, at that time, the mandatory punishment for using a firearm in the commission of a violent felony was three years in prison. During that year, Jeb Bush, in his campaign for governor of Florida, proposed the **"10-20-Life" law**. The law was enacted the following year, taking effect on July 1, 1999. It focuses primarily on the possession or use of a firearm during the commission of a crime, regardless of whether or not the weapon is an integral element of the crime. It applies to all offenders, including those who have no prior arrests or convictions. The law amended FS 775.087(2) to require minimum mandatory terms of imprisonment for crimes involving firearms.

Basically, under 10-20-Life, a felony offender who uses a firearm during the commission of one of the felonies enumerated in FS §775.087(2) will receive a mandatory minimum sentence of ten years. If the offender discharges the firearm ("pulls the trigger"), the mandatory minimum sentence is increased to twenty years, even if no one was actually injured. Finally, if the offender actually shoots someone, causing death or great bodily harm, the offender will receive a mandatory minimum sentence of imprisonment for 25 years to life (regardless of whether the offender actually lives or dies). Offenders sentenced under 10-20-Life are not eligible for parole.

The law also includes a mandatory minimum three-year prison sentence for any felony offender who possessed a gun, regardless of whether or not the offender actually used the gun during a crime. In addition, there is a special provision for offenders who commit a serious felony while possessing a machine gun or semiautomatic weapon. Possession of a machine gun during the commission (or attempted commission) of a serious felony results in a minimum mandatory sentence of fifteen years (rather than ten).

Although these terms of incarceration are mandatory, they are minimum sentences. The statute does not prohibit the court from imposing a longer sentence of incarceration, or a sentence of death, if those sentences are authorized by law. In addition, defendants sentenced under the 10-20-Life law are not eligible to have their sentences suspended or deferred, nor are they eligible for any statutory gain time or any form of discretionary early release (other than a pardon, executive clemency, or conditional medical release) until they have served the minimum sentence.

According to the Florida Department of Corrections, this law has had a significant impact on rates of violent gun crimes. Statewide, violent gun crimes have decreased by 25 percent between 1998 and 2002. In addition, 343 fewer people were killed by armed offenders in 2002 than in 1998.[16]

The law is currently under attack by opponents who feel that it is too severe. Specifically, many critics feel that the law should not apply to offenders who steal a weapon during the commission of a non-violent crime, such as a burglary.[17]

As of October 1, 2002, the 10-20-Life law was extended to cover 16- and 17-year-old offenders. See Chapter 9 for a discussion of how this law applies to juveniles.

OTHER SENTENCING ALTERNATIVES

Intermediate Sentences

Intermediate sentences are punishments that generally are harsher than probation but less punitive than a state prison sentence. According to FS 921.187(1), alternative sentences "shall be used in a manner that will best serve the needs of society, punish criminal offenders, and provide the opportunity for rehabilitation." FS 921.187(1)(a) outlines a series of alternative sentences that may be imposed if the offender does not receive a state prison sentence. These include:

- a split sentence
- probation
- probation and a fine
- community control with intensive supervision
- participation in an in-patient drug or other treatment program
- imprisonment in a county jail
- participation in a work-release, educational, or technical training program while serving time in a county jail
- participation in a substance abuse program
- payment of additional assessments
- split probation
- participation in an adult general education program with the goal of achieving functional literacy
- participation in an adult general education program with the goal of obtaining a general high school equivalency diploma
- any other disposition authorized by law

Restitution and Fines

Several types of sentences require the offender to make some type of financial payment, either to the court or to the victim of the crime. A **fine** is a monetary payment that is made to the state.

Restitution involves a monetary payment made to the victim as a way of financially repaying the victim for a loss sustained as a result of the crime. The death of the victim does not end the offender's obligation to pay restitution; if the victim dies before payments are completed, all remaining payments must be made to the estate of the deceased victim.

Currently, Florida is attempting to increase the use of victim restitution by offenders. FS §775.089(1)(a) states that:

> In addition to any punishment, the court shall order the defendant to make restitution
> to the victim for:
> 1. Damage or loss caused directly or indirectly by the defendant's offense; and
> 2. Damage or loss related to the defendant's criminal episode,
>
> unless it finds clear and compelling reasons not to order such restitution. Restitution
> may be monetary or nonmonetary restitution...

This requirement is essentially restated in FS §921.187(3). If the court does not require the offender to make restitution as an element of the sentence, the reasons why restitution was not ordered must be stated on the record. FS §775.089(2) also outlines in detail the items for which an offender may be required to make restitution.

Criminal fines may be imposed, when a specific criminal statute does not prohibit it, for any non-capital felony offense. Essentially, the court may authorize an offender to pay a fine instead of, or in addition to, an authorized term of imprisonment. The maximum amount of the fine is determined by statute, and depends on the seriousness of the crime committed. According to FS §775.083(1),

> ...Fines for designated crimes and for noncriminal violations shall not exceed:
> (a) $15,000, when the conviction is of a life felony.
> (b) $10,000, when the conviction is of a felony of the first or second degree.
> (c) $5,000, when the conviction is of a felony of the third degree.
> (d) $1,000, when the conviction is of a misdemeanor of the first degree.
> (e) $500, when the conviction is of a misdemeanor of the second degree or a noncriminal violation.
> (f) Any higher amount equal to double the pecuniary gain derived from the offense by the offender or double the pecuniary loss suffered by the victim.
> (g) Any higher amount specifically authorized by statute.

If the offender is unable to pay the fine imposed by the court, the court may defer payment of the fine until a set date. However, if the offender is indigent, or does not have the assets needed to pay the fine, the courts have held that jail time may not be imposed for failure to pay. In addition, the U.S. Supreme Court held in the case of *Tate v. Short*[18] that an offender may not be subject to imprisonment solely because s/he is indigent. However, other alternatives, such as deferred payment schedules, may be used to enforce the payment of fines.

VICTIM RIGHTS AND SERVICES

Victim Impact Statements

A **victim impact statement** is a written report or verbal statement that is given to the sentencing judge for consideration when sentencing the defendant. The statement includes admissible evidence concerning the impact or effects of the crime upon the victim. In Florida, the impact of the crime on the victim is taken into consideration at sentencing in several ways. In addition to the use of impact statements made by the victim, one of the four primary factors considered in the sentencing guidelines is that of victim injury. If the victim has suffered any sort of physical injury or trauma, the offender receives additional sentence points added to his or her total offense score. The presentence report, which is prepared by the Department of Corrections prior to sentencing, also must include "a statement regarding the extent of the victim's loss or injury."[19]

In 1998, an amendment to Article I of the Florida State Constitution provided additional rights for crime victims. The new section states that:

> Victims of crime or their lawful representatives, including the next of kin of homicide victims, are entitled to the right to be informed, to be present, and to be heard when relevant, at all crucial stages of criminal proceedings, to the extent that these rights do not interfere with the constitutional rights of the accused.[20]

The Victims' Rights Amendment was added to the section of the Constitution that outlines the rights of accused offenders. Essentially, it creates a balance in the state Constitution by giving rights not only to offenders but to victims as well. However, it should be noted that the constitutional rights of the accused offender take precedence over the rights of the victim.

If the offender has been convicted of a felony (or has pled *nolo contendere* to any crime), the victim has the right to present either written or verbal evidence before the sentencing court. If the victim has died from causes related to the crime, the victim's next of kin may appear and present evidence. FS 921.143(1) states that the victim, or the victim's next of kin, has the right to:

(a) Appear before the sentencing court for the purpose of making a statement under oath for the record; and

(b) Submit a written statement under oath to the office of the state attorney, which statement shall be filed with the sentencing court.

The statute also addresses the allowable content of such a statement. According to FS 921.143(2):

The state attorney or any assistant state attorney shall advise all victims or, when appropriate, their next of kin that statements, whether oral or written, shall relate to the facts of the case and the extent of any harm, including social, psychological, or physical harm, financial losses, loss of earnings directly or indirectly resulting from the crime for which the defendant is being sentenced, and any matter relevant to an appropriate disposition and sentence.

If the offender has been convicted of a capital offense, the prosecution may introduce victim impact evidence during the sentencing hearing. This is in addition to any statement that may be presented by the victim's next of kin. According to FS 921.141(7):

> Once the prosecution has provided evidence of the existence of one or more aggravating circumstances ... the prosecution may introduce, and subsequently argue, victim impact evidence. Such evidence shall be designed to demonstrate the victim's uniqueness as an individual human being and the resultant loss to the community's members by the victim's death. Characterizations and opinions about the crime, the defendant, and the appropriate sentence shall not be permitted as a part of victim impact evidence.

The Right to Restitution

During the sentencing phase of a trial, the judge is required to consider imposing the requirement of restitution to the victim as an element of the sentence. This generally involves requiring the offender to pay a sum of money to the victim as reimbursement for losses due to the crime. Restitution may also be in a nonmonetary form.

The court is required to consider ordering the defendant to make restitution, in addition to any other punishment that may be imposed. Thus, restitution may be ordered even if the judge sentences the offender to a fine or a term of imprisonment in jail or prison. According to FS §775.089(1)(c), victims eligible for restitution include:

> each person who suffers property damage or loss, monetary expense, or physical injury or death as a direct or indirect result of the defendant's offense or criminal episode, and also includes the victim's estate if the victim is deceased, and the victim's next of kin if the victim is deceased as a result of the offense.

FS §775.089(2)(a) discusses for what expenses the offender may be required to make restitution. If the victim was injured as a result of the crime, these expenses may include:

- the cost of necessary medical and related professional services
- the cost of necessary physical, psychiatric, and psychological care
- the cost of necessary physical and occupational therapy and rehabilitation
- reimbursement for income lost as a result of the offense
- when applicable, the cost of necessary funeral and related services

If the victim was not physically injured as a result of the crime, the defendant may still be required to pay restitution to "reimburse the victim for income lost by the victim as a result of the offense."[21]

The Right to Compensation

In addition to restitution, victims may be eligible for **compensation** through the **Bureau of Victim Compensation.** Compensation is discussed in the **Florida Crimes Compensation Act**, which is found in FS §960.01 through FS §960.28. This act assists victims who are attempting to get assistance for financial losses that are related to a violent crime. These may include lost wages, disability, funeral expenses, loss of support, treatment expenses, and other out-of-pocket expenses that a victim may incur as a direct result of a crime injury.

Not everyone is eligible to apply for victim compensation. According to FS §960.065(1), eligibility is limited to certain categories of individuals. These include:

(a) A victim.
(b) An intervenor.
(c) A surviving spouse, parent or guardian, sibling, or child of a deceased victim or intervenor.
(d) Any other person who is dependent for his or her principal support upon a deceased victim or intervenor.

For the purposes of compensation, a victim is considered to be any individual who suffers personal injury or death as the result of the crime. In addition, any person who is under the age of 16, who was present at the scene of the crime and saw or heard the crime take place, and who suffered a psychiatric or psychological (but not physical) injury as a result of the crime is included in the category of victim.[22] An intervenor is an individual who suffers bodily injury or death while trying in a lawful manner to prevent a crime, apprehend a suspect, or to help a crime victim.[23]

The act also provides a list of individuals who are specifically identified as being ineligible for awards of compensation. These include:

- any individual who committed or aided in the commission of the crime for which compensation is being claimed

- any individual who was engaged in unlawful activity at the time of the crime for which compensation is being claimed

- any individual who was confined in a detention or correctional facility at the time of the crime for which compensation is being claimed

- any individual who has been adjudicated as a habitual felony offender, habitual violent offender, or violent career criminal

- any individual who has been found guilty of a forcible felony offense.[24]

To apply for an award of compensation, the crime must have been reported to the proper authorities within 72 hours of the commission of the crime, unless the victim can show good cause for the delay in reporting.[25] In addition, an application for compensation must be filed within one year of the date of the crime, although this may be extended to two years if there is good cause.[26] According to FS §960.13(1)(a), for an award of compensation to be made, it must be shown that:

1. A crime was committed;
2. Such crime directly resulted in personal injury to, psychiatric or psychological injury to, or death of, the victim or intervenor; and
3. Such crime was promptly reported to the proper authorities.

The victim must provide proof of the crime-related expenses for which compensation is requested as well as proof of time and wages lost from work due to crime-related injuries. Compensation is intended to be the last resort for victims; only those costs which have not been reimbursed from some other source may be claimed for compensation. Therefore, if the victim has medical insurance which will cover the cost of medical care, or long-term disability insurance to cover loss of wages, the victim may not request victim compensation for these costs. Similarly, if the offender has been ordered to make restitution for some of the crime-related expenses, the victim may not apply for compensation to cover those expenses. In addition, only those expenses that are directly related to the crime may be eligible for reimbursement.

Not all crime-related expenses are covered by victims' compensation. Victim compensation benefits are available for the following expenses:

- lost wages for a victim who missed work as a result of the crime

- lost wages for a parent or guardian who missed work to care for a minor child who was a crime victim

- loss of support for dependants of a deceased victim who earned an income at the time of the crime

- a disability allowance for a victim who is disabled as a result of the crime

- funeral and related expenses for a deceased victim

- necessary medical and non-medical treatment expenses

- the cost of prescriptions, eyeglasses, prosthetics, or dentures required as a result of the crime

- the cost of mental health counseling

- reimbursement for lost property only if the victim is at least 60 years of age or a disabled adult

- relocation expenses for victims of domestic violence who have a certified and immediate need to move to a safe environment.[27]

As noted above, compensation is only given to victims who suffered injury or death as a result of the crime. Victims of property crimes are not eligible for compensation and victims of personal crimes will not, with the few exceptions noted in this list, receive compensation for property that was lost or damaged during the crime.

Obviously, the Bureau of Victim Compensation does not have an unlimited budget. Therefore, the state has placed limits on the amount of compensation that may be received by each victim. These limits are specifically stated in FS 960.13(9)(a), which states that:

> An award may not exceed:
> 1. Ten thousand dollars for treatment;
> 2. Ten thousand dollars for continuing or periodic mental health care of a minor victim whose normal emotional development is adversely affected by being the victim of a crime;
> 3. A total of $25,000 for all compensable costs; or
> 4. Fifty thousand dollars when the department makes a written finding that the victim has suffered a catastrophic injury as a direct result of the crime.

In addition, elderly victims and disabled adults who suffer a property loss that significantly affects their quality of life may qualify for an award of up to $500, under FS 960.195.

NOTES

1. Fla.R.Cr.P. 3.700(b)
2. *Florida's Criminal Punishment Code: A Comparative Assessment: A Report to the Florida Legislature Detailing Florida's Criminal Punishment Code, October 2001.* Available online at http://www.dc.state.fl.us/pub/sg_annual/0001/index.html
3. FS §921.0001
4. *Heggs v. State,* 759 So. 2d 620 (Fla. 2000)
5. Florida Parole Commission, Frequently Asked Questions (http://www.state.fl.us/fpc/FAQ.html)
6. FS §921.0024
7. FS §921.0021(4)
8. FS §921.0021(5)
9. FS §921.0023

10. FS §921.0021(3)
11. FS §921.0021(6)
12. The Law Enforcement Protection Act refers to violent crimes committed against law enforcement officers, corrections officers, state attorneys, assistant state attorneys, judges, or justices.
13. FS §921.0026(3)
14. FS §921.141
15. Florida Department of Corrections (2003). *10-20-Life Criminals Sentenced to Florida's Prisons: October 2003.* Available online at: http://www.dc.state.fl.us/pub/10-20-life/index.html
16. *Ibid*
17. Jenkins, Colleen (2003, Dec. 5). "Delegation Stands Firm on 10-20-Life". *St. Petersburg Times.*
18. *Tate v. Short*, 401 U.S. 395 (1971)
19. FS §921.231(1)(n)
20. Florida State Constitution, Article I, Section 16(b)
21. FS §775.089(2)(b)
22. FS §960.03(13)
23. FS §960.03(9)
24. FS §960.064(2)
25. FS §960.13(1)(b)
26. FS §960.07
27. Office of the Attorney General. *Crime Victim Compensation Program.* Brochure available online at http://myfloridalegal.com/Engviccmp.pdf

CHAPTER 7

CAPITAL PUNISHMENT IN FLORIDA

THE HISTORY OF CAPITAL PUNISHMENT IN FLORIDA

In 19th century Florida, executions were carried out at the county level. The primary method used was hanging, and most executions were conducted by the county sheriff. Executions were carried out at the jail or prison in which the condemned inmate was being held. However, in 1923, the Florida State Legislature officially authorized the use of electrocution as the official method of capital punishment in Florida. The first Florida electric chair was located at Union Correctional Institution. Known as "Old Sparky," it was a three-legged oak chair built by inmates in 1923. The first inmate to be electrocuted in the chair was Frank Johnson, who was put to death on October 7, 1924.[1]

Between 1924 and 1964, a total of 196 inmates were executed in Florida, although there were no executions in 1929. This figure included 21 double executions, nine triple executions, and three quadruple executions. The oldest executed inmate was 59, the two youngest were both 16. Two-thirds of the executed offenders were black. There were no executions in Florida from 1964 to 1979 because of court battles relating to capital punishment[2].

On June 29, 1972, the U.S. Supreme Court case of *Furman v. Georgia*[3] challenged the constitutionality of capital punishment in the United States. The Court ruled that the death penalty, as it was administered, constituted "cruel and unusual punishment" and therefore was a violation of the Eighth Amendment of the U.S. Constitution. The cases struck down death penalty laws throughout the country. As a result of the *Furman v. Georgia* decision, 95 men and one woman had their death sentences commuted to life in prison.[4] In December 1972, the Florida State Legislature revised the death penalty statutes (FS 921.141). Four years later, on January 15, 1976, the Court ruled in the case of *Gregg v. Georgia*[5] that capital punishment did not invariably violate the Constitution and reinstated the death penalty. On July 2, 1976, in the case of *Proffitt v. Florida*[6], the Court upheld the revised Florida statutes. The first inmate executed in Florida under the new statutes was John Spenkelink, who was put to death on May 25, 1979.[7]

Probably one of the most notorious offenders to die in the Florida electric chair was Theodore Bundy who had confessed to 31 murders in nine states. Ted Bundy was put to death on January 23, 1989.

In 1999, a new electric chair, also constructed by inmates, was built to replace the original chair built in 1923. While the wooden structure of the chair was new, the equipment that actually sends the electric current to the inmate was not altered. This equipment is tested regularly to make certain it is working properly. The new chair was installed at the Florida State Prison in Starke, Florida[7].

THE MOVE TO LETHAL INJECTION

In the 1990s, several flawed executions in Florida created serious problems for the state legislature and the Department of Corrections. The first was the execution of Jesse Tafero on May 4, 1990; the second was the execution of Pedro Medina on March 25, 1997. In both cases, flames and smoke flared up from beneath the headpiece worn by the inmates. Later investigation found that, in both cases, the improper use of sponges in the headpiece was to blame. In the Tafero execution, a synthetic sponge, which had been substituted for the natural sponge normally used, caught fire. During Medina's electrocution, one of the two sponges located inside the headpiece had not been soaked in saline solution. As a result, the dry sponge ignited. In the latter case, Florida Governor Lawton Chiles reported that investigating pathologists concluded that Medina died immediately and felt no pain from the igniting of the sponge.[9]

As a result of the Medina case, Florida began serious discussion as to whether the use of electrocution as a method of death should continue. Florida Circuit Court Judge A.C. Soud ruled in July 1997 that the electric chair was in "good working order" and did not constitute cruel or unusual punishment.[9] In October, the Florida Supreme Court, in a four-to-three ruling, upheld the decision of the lower court. However, five of the seven justices suggested that the state legislators consider the use of lethal injection.

The state legislature listened to the advice of the Florida Supreme Court. In March 1998, the legislature enacted FS §922.105, which confirmed electrocution as the method of execution used in Florida but designated lethal injection as the method to be used if the Florida Supreme Court or the United States Supreme Court ever ruled electrocution to be unconstitutional.

In November 1998, state voters approved an amendment to the state constitution which put the death penalty in the Florida Constitution and changed the constitutional prohibition against "cruel or unusual punishment" to "cruel and unusual punishment." The new constitutional provision states that:

> ...The death penalty is an authorized punishment for capital crimes designated by the Legislature ... Any method of execution shall be allowed, unless prohibited by the United States Constitution. Methods of execution may be designated by the Legislature, and a change in any method of execution may be applied retroactively. A sentence of death shall not be reduced on the basis that a method of execution is invalid. In any case in which an execution method is declared invalid, the death sentence shall remain in force until the sentence can be lawfully executed by any valid method...[10]

On July 8, 1999, another inmate, Allan Lee Davis, was being put to death when blood was observed to be seeping out from under the headpiece covering his face. After an investigation, authorities stated that Davis suffered a nosebleed which began before the electric current was applied. Despite this, the state Supreme Court stopped the next execution, which had been scheduled for July 9, and ordered a hearing into the use of the electric chair. In August, a circuit judge ruled that the state's electric chair was not cruel and unusual punishment and, in September, the state Supreme Court ruled for the second time in two years that death in the Florida electric chair did not constitute cruel and unusual punishment and thus did not violate the state Constitution.

In January 2000, during a three-day special session of the Florida State Legislature, state legislators enacted the Death Penalty Reform Act. This resulted in the adoption of lethal injection as the primary method of execution in Florida. However, because the Legislature did not abolish the use of electrocution, inmates who prefer death by electrocution may still opt for the electric chair. FS 922.105(1) was revised to state that "A death sentence shall be executed by lethal injection, unless the person sentenced to death affirmatively elects to be executed by electrocution." Essentially, an inmate who has been sentenced to death for a capital crime is given one opportunity to inform the warden of the correctional facility, in writing, that s/he chooses to have the death sentence carried out by electrocution.

As a result of the acceptance of lethal injection as a method of execution in Florida, the execution chamber was modified so that it could be used for either electrocution or lethal injection. When the chamber is used for lethal injection, the electric chair is unbolted from the floor and moved outside, although the electrical apparatus is not moved.[11]

The first execution by lethal injection in Florida occurred on February 23, 2000 when Terry Sims was put to death.

CAPITAL PUNISHMENT IN FLORIDA TODAY

According to the Florida Department of Corrections website, as of December 26, 2003, there were a total of 365 inmates on death row. This number includes 229 white males, 125 black males, 10 males of other races, and one white female.[12] The average age of inmates on death row is 41.6 years. The youngest male inmate on death row was born in 1970 and the oldest was born in 1927. The single female on death row was born in 1952.

Between 1979, three years after the death penalty was reinstated, and 2003, a total of 57 individuals have been executed in Florida. Three death row inmates were executed in 2003, and three in 2002. Florida has executed more than four people in one year only twice since 1976. In 1984, eight people were executed and in 2000, six were executed.[13]

The average length of stay on death row prior to execution is 11.76 years. The average inmate on death row was approximately 30 years old at the time of his or her offense. The youngest inmates ever executed were both 16 years old: Willie Clay was executed in 1941 and James Davis in 1944. The oldest inmate ever executed was Charlie Grifford, who was 72 years of age when he was executed in 1951. The first woman to be executed in Florida's electric chair was Judias ("Judy") Buenoano, who was electrocuted on March 30, 1998. Buenoano was executed for the murder of her paralyzed son.[14]

In 1994, the Florida Supreme Court ruled that the execution of an offender who was 15 at the time of the crime constitutes cruel or unusual punishment and was a violation of the state Constitution. In 1998, the Court held that the execution of an offender who was 16 years of age at the time of the crime also violated the constitutional protection against cruel or unusual punishment. Currently, the minimum age for the imposition of the death penalty in Florida is 17.[15]

As of 2001, Florida no longer allows defendants charged with capital crimes to be executed if they are mentally retarded. However, the law is not retroactive. Mentally retarded defendants sentenced to death prior to the effective date of the new law may still be put to death.[16] To be defined as mentally retarded, an individual must receive a score of less than 70 on an I.Q. test.[17]

LAWS RELATING TO A SENTENCE OF DEATH IN FLORIDA

Death penalty trials are discussed in Chapter 921 of the Florida Statutes. Florida uses a bifurcated procedure, so that the determination of guilt or innocence and the sentencing decision occur at separate proceedings. According to FS 921.141, for a sentence of death to be imposed, several conditions must be met. The offender must first be convicted or adjudicated guilty of a capital felony. At this point, the court must hold a separate sentencing proceeding to determine whether the offender will receive a sentence of life imprisonment or death. When possible, the sentencing hearing will involve the trial judge and the trial jury. If the defendant pleaded guilty, or waived his or her right to a jury trial, a jury will be impaneled for the purpose of sentencing. However, the defendant does have the right to waive his or her right to a jury in the sentencing proceeding.[18]

Fla. R. Crim. P. 3.780 outlines the procedures for a sentencing hearing in a capital case. Both the state and the defendant are allowed to present evidence regarding aggravating and mitigating circumstances. The state presents its evidence first, followed by the defense. Each side may present witnesses and each may cross-examine those witnesses presented by the other side. Rebuttal is also permitted. Opening and closing arguments are also allowed, with the state again going first.

During the sentencing proceeding, the court must consider both aggravating and mitigating circumstances. A sentence of death may only be imposed if "sufficient aggravating circumstances exist... and... there are insufficient mitigating circumstances to outweigh the aggravating circumstances." After the jury hears the evidence presented by both the defense and the state, it will deliberate and render a verdict to the judge. This is an advisory sentence only and the judge is not bound to accept it.[19]

There are a total of fourteen aggravating circumstances, which are listed in FS 921.141(5). These include:

(a) The capital felony was committed by a person previously convicted of a felony and under sentence of imprisonment or placed on community control or on felony probation.

(b) The defendant was previously convicted of another capital felony or of a felony involving the use or threat of violence to the person.

(c) The defendant knowingly created a great risk of death to many persons.

(d) The capital felony was committed while the defendant was engaged, or was an accomplice, in the commission of, or an attempt to commit, or flight after committing or attempting to commit, any: robbery; sexual battery; aggravated child abuse; abuse of an elderly person or disabled adult resulting in great bodily harm, permanent disability, or permanent disfigurement; arson; burglary; kidnapping; aircraft piracy; or unlawful throwing, placing, or discharging of a destructive device or bomb.

(e) The capital felony was committed for the purpose of avoiding or preventing a lawful arrest or effecting an escape from custody.

(f) The capital felony was committed for pecuniary gain.

(g) The capital felony was committed to disrupt or hinder the lawful exercise of any governmental function or the enforcement of laws.

(h) The capital felony was especially heinous, atrocious, or cruel.

(i) The capital felony was a homicide and was committed in a cold, calculated, and premeditated manner without any pretense of moral or legal justification.

(j) The victim of the capital felony was a law enforcement officer engaged in the performance of his or her official duties.

(k) The victim of the capital felony was an elected or appointed public official engaged in the performance of his or her official duties if the motive for the capital felony was related, in whole or in part, to the victim's official capacity.

(l) The victim of the capital felony was a person less than 12 years of age.

(m) The victim of the capital felony was particularly vulnerable due to advanced age or disability, or because the defendant stood in a position of familial or custodial authority over the victim.

(n) The capital felony was committed by a criminal street gang member...

In addition, FS 921.141(6) outlines the eight mitigating circumstances that may be considered by the court. These include:

(a) The defendant has no significant history of prior criminal activity.

(b) The capital felony was committed while the defendant was under the influence of extreme mental or emotional disturbance.

(c) The victim was a participant in the defendant's conduct or consented to the act.

(d) The defendant was an accomplice in the capital felony committed by another person and his or her participation was relatively minor.

(e) The defendant acted under extreme duress or under the substantial domination of another person.

(f) The capacity of the defendant to appreciate the criminality of his or her conduct or to conform his or her conduct to the requirements of law was substantially impaired.

(g) The age of the defendant at the time of the crime.

(h) The existence of any other factors in the defendant's background that would mitigate against imposition of the death penalty.

If the prosecution has produced evidence to show that at least one aggravating factor exists, Florida state law allows for the introduction of victim impact evidence, which is "designed to demonstrate the victim's uniqueness as an individual human being and the resultant loss to the community's members by the victim's death."[20]

FLORIDA'S DEATH ROW

Florida's Death Row for male inmates is currently located in the Florida State Prison in Starke. The standard death row cell is 6 feet wide, 9 feet long, and 9.5 feet high. In addition, the prison has death watch cells which hold inmates who are awaiting execution after the state governor has signed the death warrant. The death watch cells are 12 feet wide, 7 feet long, and 8.5 feet high. In addition, some inmates awaiting execution are housed at the Union Correctional Institution in Raiford, Florida. Women inmates awaiting execution are housed at the Lowell Correctional Institution, located in Lowell, Florida. As of December 2003, it cost approximately $72.39 per day to incarcerate an inmate on death row.[21]

Death row inmates are served three meals a day; breakfast at 5:00 a.m., lunch between 10:30 and 11:00 a.m., and dinner from 4:00 to 4:30 p.m. Meals are prepared by prison personnel and transported to the inmates' cells in insulated carts. Death row inmates do not eat with the general prison population. The inmate's "last meal," which may be requested prior to execution, must be purchased locally and may not cost more than $20.

Death row inmates may receive visitors every weekend between 9:00 a.m. and 3:00 p.m. although all visitors must be approved in advance by prison officials before they are placed on the inmate's official visitor list. Visitors who must travel over 200 miles may visit on both Saturday and Sunday. If a member of the news media wants to interview a death row inmate, s/he must request such an interview through the Florida Department of Corrections. Media interviews are non-contact, and the inmate must agree to the interview.

Inmates receive mail daily (except holidays and weekends) and may have snack foods, cigarettes, radios, and black-and-white televisions in their cells. They may also smoke in their cells. Although the use of tobacco is banned inside Florida prisons, death row inmates are exempt because they have no access to designated smoking areas. There is no air conditioning or cable television in death row. The inmates are not allowed to socialize together at any time in a common room. This includes communal religious services; inmates watch church services in their cells on closed-circuit televison. While the inmates are on death watch, they may have radios and black-and-white televisions positioned outside the bars of the cell but may not bring them into the death watch cell.

Security is a constant feature of death row. Inmates on death row are counted at least once every hour. Whenever they leave their cells they are escorted in handcuffs; death row inmates wear handcuffs everywhere except in their cells, the shower, and the exercise yard. They do not leave their cells except for exercise, medical reasons, visits, or media interviews. They wear the same blue pants as regular inmates but are easily identified by their orange t-shirts.[22]

THE PROCEDURE FOR EXECUTIONS IN FLORIDA

The Death Chamber

All executions are held in the death chamber at Florida State Prison. The chamber is a small room, 12 feet by 15 feet. It can be used for either electrocution or lethal injection. The chamber contains the oak electric chair, which is bolted to the floor and sits on a rubber mat for extra insulation. In addition, there are two telephones in the room; one is for the institution, the other is for the governor in case of a last-minute stay of execution. When the chamber is used for lethal injection, the wooden chair is unbolted and moved outside the room. The electrical apparatus is not moved. For execution by lethal injection, the inmate is transported into and out of the death chamber on a wheeled gurney.

The death chamber is separated from the witness room by a glass partition. The room for witnesses can accommodate 22 seats. The state requires the presence of twelve official witnesses, who are selected by the warden. The remaining ten seats are generally reserved for news reporters.

Electrocutions

Executions are generally held at 7:00 a.m. because inmates are already in lock-down awaiting the 8:00 a.m. administrative shift change and therefore the prison is more secure at this time. Prior to the late 1990s, there was no formal written procedure for executions in Florida.

The usual procedure begins approximately one hour before the execution when the inmate's head and right calf are shaved, along with a patch on the chest. The inmate is allowed to shower and then returns to the holding cell. The death warrant is read aloud by the superintendent of the prison. The electrolytic gel is applied to the inmate's head and right calf and s/he is taken to the death chamber and strapped into the electric chair. The inmate's head is covered with a leather hood lined with wool, which was also made at the prison. According to FS §922.10, the executioner is appointed by the warden of the Florida State Prison and his or her identity remains anonymous. S/he is a private citizen, not a correctional officer. The executioner's sole task is to turn the switch on the control panel next to the electric chair at a signal (usually a nod) from the prison superintendent. Flipping this switch begins the automated electrocution cycle. The electrocution itself takes less than two minutes.

Lethal Injections

Like electrocutions, lethal injections in Florida are held early in the morning. The early stages of the procedure are similar to those involved during an electrocution, although the inmate's head and calf are not shaved. Immediately prior to execution, as required by FS §922.10, the death warrant is read aloud to the offender. The inmate will be offered Valium as a calming agent. S/he is then strapped to a gurney and an intravenous (IV) line is put into each arm. The inmate is then wheeled into the death chamber and is allowed to make a final statement. After the warden checks with the governor for a last-second stay of execution, a hooded executioner begins the procedure of lethal injection. The inmate is first injected through the IV tube with two syringes of sodium pentothal, which places the inmate into a deep sleep. The inmate is next injected with two syringes of pancuronium bromide, which paralyzes the muscles and stops breathing, generally within one to three minutes. Last, the inmate is injected with two syringes of potassium chloride which will stop his or her heart. The entire procedure is supervised by a physician who makes the final pronouncement of death. The entire procedure takes between 10 and 15 minutes. According to FS §922.106, the identity of the individual who administers the lethal injection is to remain confidential.

NOTES

1.   Florida Department of Corrections, Death Row Fact Sheet
      (http://www.dc.state.fl.us/oth/deathrow)
2.   *Ibid*
3.   *Furman v. Georgia*, 408 U.S. 238 (1972)
4.   Florida Department of Corrections, Death Row Fact Sheet, *op cit.*

5.   *Gregg v. Georgia*, 428 U.S. 153 (1976)
6.   *Proffit v. Florida*, 428 U.S. 325 (1976)
7.   Florida Department of Corrections, Death Row Fact Sheet, *op cit.*
8.   "Statement by Governor Lawton Chiles Regarding Diagnostic Test on Florida's Electric Chair", April 11, 1997
(http://www.eog.state.fl.us/eog/govdocs/presrele/1997/apr97/4-11chai.html)
9.   *Jones v. Butterworth*, 691 So.2d 481 (Fla. 1997)
10.   Florida State Constitution, Article I, §17
11.   Florida Department of Corrections, DOC Planning for Lethal Injection, January 26, 2000
(http://www.dc.state.fl.us/secretary/press/2000/injection.html)
12.   Florida Department of Corrections, Death Row Roster
(http://www.dc.state.fl.us/activeinmates/deathrowroster.asp)
13.   Florida Department of Corrections, Death Row Fact Sheet, *op cit.*
14.   *Ibid*
15.   Death Penalty Information Center (http://www.deathpenaltyinfo.org/)
16.   FS §921.137
17.   Florida Department of Corrections, Florida Corrections: Centuries of Progress
(http://www.dc.state.fl.us/oth/timeline/index.html)
18.   http://www.dc.state.fl.us/oth/timeline/2000-2002.html
19.   FS §921.141(3)
20.   FS §921.141(2) and (3)
21.   FS §921.141(7)
22.   Florida Department of Corrections, Death Row Fact Sheet, *op cit.*
23.   *Ibid*

CHAPTER 8

CORRECTIONS IN FLORIDA

INTRODUCTION

The **Florida Department of Corrections** oversees the operation of all correctional facilities in the state. As of June 30, 2003, Florida had 123 correctional facilities, including 56 prisons (five of which are privately run under contract), 36 work or forestry camps, 24 work release centers, five road prisons, and two treatment centers.[1]

The **Florida Corrections Commission** was established in 1994 by the Florida State Legislature. According to FS 20.315(6)(b), the Commission's primary functions are to:

1. Recommend major correctional policies for the Governor's approval, and assure that approved policies and any revisions thereto are properly executed.
2. Periodically review the status of the state correctional system and recommend improvements therein to the Governor and the Legislature.
3. Annually perform an in-depth review of community-based intermediate sanctions and recommend to the Governor and the Legislature intergovernmental approaches through the Community Corrections Partnership Act for planning and implementing such sanctions and programs.
4. Perform an in-depth evaluation of the annual budget request of the Department of Corrections, the comprehensive correctional master plan, and the tentative construction program for compliance with all applicable laws and established departmental policies. The commission may not consider individual construction projects, but shall consider methods of accomplishing the department's goals in the most effective, efficient, and businesslike manner.
5. Routinely monitor the financial status of the Department of Corrections to assure that the department is managing revenue and any applicable bond proceeds responsibly and in accordance with law and established policy.
6. Evaluate, at least quarterly, the efficiency, productivity, and management of the Department of Corrections, using performance and production standards developed by the department...
7. Provide public education on corrections and criminal justice issues.
8. Report to the President of the Senate, the Speaker of the House of Representatives, and the Governor by November 1 of each year...

The Commission is composed of nine members who are appointed by the Governor and confirmed by the Senate. They are appointed in such a way as to equally represent all areas of the state. To serve on the Commission, an individual must be a United States citizen and a registered voter of the state of Florida. Commission members are unpaid volunteers who serve four-year terms.

Because the Commission's purpose is to oversee the state's correctional system, it functions for the most part independently of the Florida Department of Corrections.[2]

A HISTORY OF CORRECTIONS IN FLORIDA

The Florida Department of Corrections website contains a history of corrections in the state of Florida, focusing on the development of the Department but also including a look at the entire system of corrections in the state.[13]

In 1868, the Chattahoochee Arsenal officer's quarters was converted into the state's first prison. The first recorded inmate, Calvin Williams, was convicted of larceny in November 1868 and received a sentence of one year in prison. By the following year, the prison population increased to 42 inmates. In addition, the institution also housed insane individuals. Inmates at Chattahoochee worked eight hours per day, six days per week. The prison allowed for inmates to earn reductions in their sentences in two ways. First, for each month in which an inmate was not punished, his sentence was reduced by three days. Second, inmates who performed their work well and did not violate prison rules could qualify for a reduction of an additional five days off each month.

In 1877, under then-governor George Franklin Drew, Florida began using the **convict-lease system**. Under this system, prisoners were leased to individuals and private corporations. The individual or company leasing the prisoner paid the state a fee and was required to provide clothing, food, housing, and medical care for the prisoner. Leased inmates worked in a wide variety of industries, including farming, logging, phosphate mining, railroad building, sawmilling and turpentining. Originally, the fee per convict was $26 per year. However, this was increased over time to $150 per year. Inmates lived in work or road camps and often were treated brutally and inhumanely.

In 1913, the **Raidford State Penitentiary** was built. It was known by a variety of names, including the "State Prison Farm," "Raidford Prison," and "Florida State Prison." Originally, it housed offenders who could not be leased, generally due to age and/or infirmity. However, over the years it expanded to become the largest correctional institution in the state. By 1919, in addition to the prison farm, it also included garment and shoe factories.

In 1919, there were 485 inmates in Florida. In that year, the state began to use inmates on **chain gangs** to build and maintain public roadways throughout the state. Inmates wore leg irons and were supervised by armed correctional officers. Although inmates on chain gangs were separated by race, and if they suffered from tuberculosis, inmates convicted of minor crimes were not segregated from the mentally ill or from those serving life sentences. Even after the convict-lease system was abolished in 1923, chain gangs continued to be a common sight on Florida roads.

The number of prison industries increased in the 1920s. In 1927, the state opened a shirt factory and an automobile license tag factor. The prison population in that year rose to over 2,500 inmates. At the same time, the warden of the State Prison Farm managed to cut costs by approximately 50 percent. By 1932, the prison population increased to over 3,200 inmates. Of these, approximately 2,000 were housed at Raidford Prison Farm while the rest were assigned to work camps, road prisons, or other facilities. The second prison farm was opened in that year in Belle Glade, Florida. In 1961, this facility was renamed the Glades Correctional Institution. Also in 1932, the Raidford Prison Farm got a new warden, Leonard Chapmen, who would serve in this position for 25 years. Under his guidance, the word "convict"was replaced with "inmates" and correctional officers were required to wear official uniforms. He replaced the solid barriers around the prison with chain-link fences, allowing inmates to see outside the facility, and discontinued the striped inmate uniforms. He also began new inmate training programs in plumbing, automobile mechanics, carpentry, printing and millwork, as well as providing grade school classes for inmates.

In 1941, the Florida State Constitution was amended to create the **Florida Parole and Probation Commission**. The three-member Commission was responsible for granting parole and for supervising offenders on probation and parole. Selection of the Commission members ws done on merit and in its first full year of operation, the Commission granted parole to 625 individuals. Another 335 offenders were placed on probation by the courts. All these offenders were supervised by the Commission.

In December, 1941, the inmate population was almost 3,800. However, by the end of 1944, this number had dropped to 2,415, possibly due in part to World War II. Inmates participated in the war effort by addressing and mailing ration books to Floridians, and by contributing approximately $12,000 towards the purchase of war bonds in 1943.

By 1949, the inmate population had risen to over 3,800. In that year the Apalachee Correctional Institution-East Unit was built in Sneads, Florida. This facility housed youthful male offenders and was the first in Florida to focus on a special inmate population. In 1956, the first women's prison, the Florida Correctional Institution, was built in Lowell, Florida. The following year the state opened another prison for adult males, the Avon Park Correctional Institution. During the next decades, prison building continued and a number of additional prisons and road camp facilities were constructed. In 1968, Florida established the first reception center, designed to screen and classify inmates, and determine which correctional facility is most appropriate for each individual inmate.

By 1969, the inmate population had risen to over 8,400 inmates. The Division of Corrections had seven prisons and 19 road camps and employed almost 2,600 individuals. During the next decade, more women and minorities were employed in correctional facilities, and began to hold positions of responsibility. Overcrowding was a serious problem in the 1970s; the inmate population had more than doubled, reaching 19,995 by 1979. The overcrowding problem was temporarily solved in 1975 by housing inmates in tents, but the courts held that this was unacceptable, leaving the prisons more crowded than before. In November 1978, there were a number of escapes from Florida correctional institutions, including one escape from the Florida State Prison death row on November

18. The escapee, Robert Fieldmore Lewis, was recaptured eleven days later by the FBI in South Carolina.

Overcrowding continued to be a serious problem in the 1980s. Between 1980 and 1989, the prison population in Florida increased from 19,692 to over 38,000. Much of the approximately 93 percent increase was due to the appearance of crack cocaine. 1980 was not a good year for Florida State Prison. In August, ten inmates escaped through holes cut in the recreation yard fence. In October, a corrections officer was fatally stabbed while escorting death row inmates to the shower, and another was stabbed but not killed. Two correctional officers were taken hostage and only released after the inmate is shot by another officer. During the same week, inmates created a variety of disturbances, including flooding their cells, breaking windows, and burning mattresses. The following year, there were two separate hostage situations at another Florida prison, Union Correctional Institution, and five escapes from Florida State Prison.

In 1982, the Legislature created a special **Corrections Overcrowding Task Force**. In 1983, the Task Force presented a set of 57 recommendations to the Legislature and then-Governor Bob Graham. As a result, the Correctional Reform Act of 1983 was passed, authorizing a mechanism for emergency release of offenders when the prison population reaches 98 percent of capacity. The state also began using house arrest, an alternative to incarceration, to reduce the overcrowding problem. The state also discontinued parole for all offenders sentenced after October 1, 1983 and implemented the first sentencing guidelines.

Despite the recommendations of the Task Force, and efforts of the Division of Corrections, overcrowding continued to be a serious problem. The state focused on building more prisons. Between 1987 and 1997, the state appropriated money for over 53,000 additional prison beds in new prisons and work camps. In addition, several drug treatment centers were opened in the early 1990s to hold the increasing number of drug offenders entering the correctional system. Another attempt to reduce the overcrowding problem came in 1983, with the establishment of the **Florida Correctional Privatization Commission**. The Commission focused on contracting with private corporations to build and operate prisons at a lower cost than the state. By 2003, there were five private correctional facilities in Florida: three adult male facilities, one youthful male offender facility, and one female facility.

In 1994, the state created the **Florida Department of Juvenile Justice**. Among the responsibilities of this new agency was the operation of juvenile justice institutions and facilities and the supervision of juvenile offenders. Some offenders were diverted out of the state prison system into the Department of Juvenile Justice, but juvenile offenders who were sentenced as adults continued to be placed in the adult prison system.

The following year, legislation was passed requiring offenders to serve a minimum of 85 percent of their sentence. The law applied to all offenders committing crimes on or after October 1, 1995, and resulted from an increased desire for "truth in sentencing." By 1998, the average percentage of a sentence served by inmates was 74 percent, more than twice that of inmates released in 1992. This figure had not yet reached 85 percent, because more than half of all inmates in prison in 1998 had not been sentenced under the 85 percent law. The percentage of sentence served continued to increase annually.

In 1999, the Three Strikes Violent Offenders Act and the 10-20-Life Law were passed, resulting in increased prison terms for certain classes of offenders. This obviously affected the prison population, which increased to over 77,000 by June 2003. While the inmate population in Florida is still on the rise, the rate of increase appears to have slowed significantly. Between 1990 and 1999, the inmate population increased by 61 percent. However, between 2000 and 2003, the population has increased by only 9 percent.[14]

JAILS IN FLORIDA

In Florida, the primary difference between a **jail** and a **prison** is that prisons are usually run by the state whereas jails are managed by the county or local municipality. Inmates of state prison facilities are convicted felony offenders who have been sentenced to serve a sentence of incarceration of one year or more. Inmates in county jails may be convicted offenders serving sentences of less than one year or may be incarcerated while awaiting trial or sentencing. The average length of stay in a jail is much shorter than in a prison; some inmates may only stay a few hours whereas others may be held for several years while awaiting trial.

Jails in Florida have three main functions:

- to house those defendants awaiting trial who were not granted pretrial release

- to punish convicted offenders who are sentenced to incarceration in a local facility

- to hold inmates awaiting transfer to other facilities.

Most jails in Florida are designed as maximum security facilities because they must be able to accommodate all arrested offenders, regardless of the charges against them. Jails provide a wide range of medical and mental health services as well as operating programs such as work release and boot camps. They also provide programs to address issues such as vocational and substance abuse needs and provide referrals to link inmates to local community programs upon release.

In 2002, county detention facilities in Florida had an average daily population of 53,499, a 10.4 percent increase over the 2001 inmate population. Of these, approximately 86 percent were adult males, 12 percent were adult females, 1.6 percent were juvenile males, and 0.1 percent were juvenile females. This distribution has not changed significantly in the last eight years. Approximately 73 percent of inmates were incarcerated for felony offenses and 20 percent for misdemeanor offenses. Most of the juveniles (over 78 percent) were charged with felony offenses. Approximately 57 percent of offenders housed in county facilities were not convicted of a crime but were detained awaiting trial.[3]

Miami-Dade County Corrections and Rehabilitation Department

The **Miami-Dade County Corrections and Rehabilitation Department** is the largest county correctional facility in the state of Florida and is larger than many state-wide correctional systems in the United States. It includes five facilities which hold, on average, 7,000 inmates per day. Inmates held in these facilities may be pretrial detainees or may be convicted offenders serving sentences of less than one year.[4] As of June 30, 2002, the Department employed 1,987 full-time certified correctional officers.[5]

The **Pre-Trial Detention Center** has space for over 1,700 inmates. It serves as a booking facility to process and house all types of inmates, ranging from minor misdemeanor offenders to those charged with capital crimes. The **Metro West Correctional Center** is the largest facility in the Department, with almost 3,100 beds. This facility houses male inmates at all custody levels. The **Training and Treatment Center** holds adult males convicted of felonies or misdemeanors and has space for over 1,300 inmates. The **Turner Guilford Knight Correctional Center** has space for 1,300 male and female offenders. Finally, the **Women's Detention Center** has 375 beds and houses both pre-trial detainees and sentenced female offenders. In addition, the Department operates a **Boot Camp** for youthful male and female offenders between the ages of 14 and 28 who have been adjudicated as adults. Inmates who, for medical reasons, cannot be housed at any of these facilities are housed in the Department's **Hospital Services Unit** which is located in Ward D of Jackson Medical Center.[6]

Broward County Jail System

The **Broward Sheriff's Office** (BSO) runs the 13th largest local jail system in the country. It is one of the few jail systems in the United States to receive national accreditation from the American Correctional Association's Commission on Accreditation for Corrections. In addition, it has also received state accreditation from Florida's Corrections Accreditation Commission.[7] The BSO was reaccredited by the American Correctional Association in January 2002.[8]

The BSO's **Department of Detention & Community Control** operates a total of four jail facilities and books in approximately 77,000 inmates each year. The Department has an average daily population of over 4,600 inmates, including those on work release. In addition, the **Transportation Bureau** is responsible for moving almost 250,000 inmates each year, taking them to court appearances, state facilities, and between county detention facilities.[9]

The **Main Jail** is an adult male maximum security facility located in downtown Fort Lauderdale, Florida, next to the county courthouse. It has bed space for 1,548 inmates. The majority of the inmates housed in the Main Jail are awaiting trial and are considered to be in need of a maximum security facility because they are seen as violent or dangerous, at high risk of escape, or because of the nature of the charges against them. The Main Jail also has space for a small number of juveniles (generally an average of about 65 at a time) who are awaiting trial in adult court. Juvenile defendants are housed separately from the adult male inmates. In addition, the Department's **Central Intake Unit** is also housed within the Main Jail Bureau and handles booking and processing for all law enforcement agencies in the county.

The **North Broward Bureau** houses both male and female adult offenders as well as some juvenile offenders. It is a minimum/medium security facility and was designed to hold 1,320 inmates. The facility houses both pre-trial detainees as well as convicted offenders serving sentences. It also includes a **Therapeutic Living Community** (TLC) program which focuses on helping inmates with substance abuse problems to become drug free. Participation in this program is voluntary. The **Joseph V. Conte Facility** is a medium-security, direct supervision facility housing male inmates, most of whom are awaiting trial. It houses 1,328 inmates and provides intensive substance abuse programs. The facility was named after Deputy Joseph V. Conte, who was killed in the line of duty in 1979. The **Stockade Facility** is a minimum/medium security jail housing both pre-trial defendants and convicted offenders. It has a capacity of almost 700 inmates and provides a variety of specialized programs to help offenders prepare for their return to the community. Finally, the BSO **Woman's Facility**, which is expected to open in 2004, will have space for over 1,000 female inmates. It is designed to be a medium/maximum security facility based on the same direct supervision model as the Conte Facility. The Women's Facility is expected to offer a variety of inmate programs, including drug rehabilitation, conflict resolution, job and life skills, and GED courses.[10] In 2002, the average daily population of the Department was 4,815. This is an average incarceration rate of 2.9 per 1,000 persons in the county.[11]

BSO operates a program in which male inmates from the Stockade Facility and female inmates from the North Broward Bureau are placed in **Work Units** and provide labor for both publicly-funded and non-profit organizations. To be eligible for participation in the program, inmates must have been convicted of a non-violent offense (minor drug charges, civil infractions, traffic violations, etc.). They must pass a medical exam, have no prior escape record, be considered a low escape risk, and have the physical ability to perform the work (generally, they must pre-qualify by demonstrating the ability to lift 50 pounds or more). Activities in which inmates participate include playground construction and repair, beach cleanups, street and road cleanup, landscape maintenance in BSO facilities and in county parks, grooming the BSO horses and maintaining the stables, and operating the BSO car wash facility. Since the early 1990s, the units have also worked with Habitat for Humanity in the building of over 125 homes and have saved the organization over $1 million. Each work unit includes four to nine inmates who are supervised by a BSO deputy. BSO estimates that these work units have saved the county over $1.2 million annually.[12]

PRISONS IN FLORIDA

Florida state prisons are run by the **Florida Department of Corrections** (DOC), whose mission is to "protect the public by operating a safe, secure, humane and efficient corrections system."[15] The department's primary goals, as stated on their web site, are to:

1. Protect the public, staff and inmates
2. Develop staff committed to professionalism and fiscal responsibility
3. Ensure victims and stakeholders are treated with dignity, sensitivity and respect in making and executing administrative and operational decisions
4. Prepare offenders for re-entry and release into society[16]

As of June 30, 2003, there were 77,316 inmates in the Florida prison system. This is an increase of 5.1 percent over the previous fiscal year and a 53 percent increase since June 1993. Of the inmates in prison on June 30, 2003, 94 percent were male and six percent were female. Approximately 53 percent were black, 45 percent were white, and 3 percent were of other races. The majority of offenders, (approximately 72 percent) were between the ages of 25 and 49. Almost 10 percent were at least 50 years of age, and there were almost 300 inmates who were under the age of 18. The youngest inmates were 14 years of age. The number of older inmates is increasing while the number of juveniles in the prison system is declining.[17]

More than half (53 percent) of all inmates incarcerated in the Florida prison system on June 30, 2003 were convicted of violent crimes. These included murder and manslaughter (14 percent), sexual offenses (11 percent), robbery (13 percent), and other violent personal crimes such as aggravated assault and carjacking (12 percent). Approximately 21 percent were convicted of property crimes, including burglary (16 percent) and theft, forgery, and fraud (8 percent). Approximately 19 percent were convicted of drug offenses, 3 percent of weapons-related offenses, and four percent of other crimes. Over 47 percent of the inmates had been committed to a Florida prison in the past. The average sentence length of current inmates was 14.9 years; the median sentence length was 7.1 years. Almost 26 percent of inmates incarcerated were serving sentences of less than three years.[18]

The DOC operates a total of 123 prison facilities. Only inmates who have been convicted of a crime (usually a felony) and sentenced to more than one year of incarceration are housed in these facilities. There are five levels of custody or security in Florida prisons. **Maximum custody** is reserved for inmates who are under a sentence of death. Offenders on **close custody** generally must stay within the secure and armed perimeter of the institution. When they are outside this secure perimeter, they must be under direct and armed supervision by a correctional officer. Offenders placed on **medium custody** may be placed in a secure perimeter work camp but not in an outside work facility which does not have armed supervision. **Minimum custody** is for offenders who are eligible to be outside an institution's secure perimeter without being under direct armed supervision. Finally, offenders classified as **community custody** are eligible to be moved out of a secure institution and placed in a community residential facility. An inmate's custody level is determined based on the level of risk the inmate represents to the public, other inmates, correctional staff, and the correctional facility.[19]

There are five main types of facilities operated by the DOC: major correctional institutions, work and forestry camps, treatment centers, work release centers, and road prisons. The 56 **major correctional institutions** operated by the DOC house about 84 percent of all state prison inmates. These are prisons which have borders protected by fences or razor wire, guard towers manned by armed correctional officers, and electronic detection systems. The majority of the inmates are housed in dormitories with bunk beds, although inmates who are confined for security or disciplinary reasons, as well as inmates on death row, are housed in cells. Most of the institutions (51) house male inmates. There are four facilities which hold only female inmates and one housing both male and female offenders. Five of the institutions are privately-contracted facilities.

The **work/forestry camps** are minimum and medium security facilities housing approximately 13 percent of the DOC population. Most inmates who are assigned to work camps have already spent some time at a major institution and have shown satisfactory progress. Most of the camps are located adjacent to major institutions, which allows them to share some facilities (e.g., health services, laundry facilities). Inmates housed in work camps may be assigned to a variety of community and public work tasks, such as painting, building construction, grounds and building maintenance, and cleaning up roadways and forests.

There are 24 **work release centers** (WRCs) which house minimum custody inmates who are participating in community work release or who have a work assignment at the center and serve as center support. To be assigned to a WRC, inmates must be within two to three years of release and may not have been convicted of a sex-related offense. Offenders who have an assignment at a WRC may work in food service, center maintenance, or transportation. Offenders participating in community work release have a paid job out in the community but live at the WRC. Community work release offenders are required to save a portion of their earnings for their release, to pay victim restitution, and to pay room and board to the center. Approximately three percent of the prison population participated in work release programs.

Finally, the five **road prisons** house less than one percent of the prison population in minimum and medium security facilities. Most of the inmates housed in road prisons work on the highways and on community work squads. They also provide a variety of support services to state agencies.[20]

When an inmate receives a sentence of incarceration for over one year, s/he is transported from the county jail to one of the state's five **reception centers**, three of which are for male offenders and two of which are for female offenders. When inmates arrive at the reception center, they are processed and tested. The program needs of each inmate are evaluated and the inmate's security risk or custody level is determined. Each inmate is then transferred to the facility which most closely meets his or her needs.

PRISON LABOR

Until the 1920s, Florida correctional institutions leased convicts to private employers. By the turn of the century, the fee paid to the state was $150 per inmate annually. However, in 1921, a 21-year-old inmate, Martin Tabert, died in a lumber company camp. Taber was a resident of North Dakota who was convicted of stealing a ride on a freight train. He was sentenced to pay a fine of $25 or be imprisoned at hard labor for three months. Although Tabert's family wired the money, the Leon County court never received it and Tabert was turned over to the Putnam Lumber Company, who paid $20 a month for the hire of convicts. When he fell ill and could not complete his work assignment, he was severely flogged by the company's whipping boss and died later that day. Tabert's death led to a national outcry against Florida's convict-leasing system and the practice was formally abolished in 1923. In addition, as a result of Tabert's death, the governor signed a bill outlawing the flogging of prisoners.[21]

The majority of inmates in Florida DOC institutions work, participate in vocational or adult education classes, or are involved in a combination of work and educational programs. A small number (less than 20 percent) do not work because they are medically unable, are participating in a DOC reception and orientation process, are assigned to a disciplinary work squad (generally because of some infraction of institution rules and regulations), or have been placed in some form of security confinement (including death row).[22] The DOC uses inmate labor to build new correctional facilities and to assist in the day-to-day operation of existing institutions. This includes preparing and serving meals, acting as prison groundskeepers, and maintaining prison farms and gardens. There are several specific programs to which inmates may be assigned, including the **Prison Rehabilitative Industries and Diversified Enterprises** (PRIDE), **Prison Industry Enhancement** (PIE), and **Community Work Squads**.

The Community Work Squad Program

Community work squads involve contracts between the DOC and other government agencies, such as the Department of Agriculture, the Department of Transportation, local and city governments, and non-profit organizations. The work squad program allows inmates to provide needed services to the community. Currently, there are three basic types of community work squads.

Department of Transportation Work Squads were created through a formal agreement between the DOC and the Florida Department of Transportation (DOT). Inmates on these squads are supervised by staff members from both agencies while performing roadway and right-of-way work which helps to maintain the Florida state highway system. In addition, if natural disasters such as hurricanes occur, DOT work squads may help with clean up and repair of damages. During fiscal year 2002-2003, inmates on the DOT work squads completed 2 million work hours valued at over $14.9 million.

Public Works and Interagency Community Service Work Squads involve local agreements between individual correctional institutions and various governmental agencies. These may include state agencies such as the Division of Forestry as well as city, county, or municipal governments and non-profit organizations. Inmates participate in public works such as roadway and right-of-way work for cities and counties, building maintenance, grounds maintenance, painting, construction, office moving, mowing, litter removal, and cleanup of state forests. In addition, upon request, these squads may assist state and local governments in clean up and repair after natural disasters. These squads are specifically authorized in FS §946.40. During FY 2002-2003, inmates on these squads completed over 3.8 million hours of work, valued at over $43 million.

Finally, **Contracted Work Squads** were authorized by the state legislature in 1997 and allow inmates to work for outside government entities who contract with the DOT to pay for inmate services. Inmates assigned to these work squads participate in similar activities as those assigned to public works and interagency community service work squads. At the end of FY 2002-2003, there were 37 active contracts. During that fiscal year, inmates completed over 504,000 hours of work which was valued at $5.7 million. Together, inmates in the three types of community work squads performed almost 6.4 million hours of work, valued at over $64.2 million, resulting in a net savings of approximately $35 million for Florida taxpayers.[23]

Prison Industry Enhancement Programs

The **Prison Industry Enhancement (PIE) Program** provides inmates with employment opportunities that are similar to private sector jobs. The program allows private industry to employ inmate labor and sell the products produced through interstate commerce. Industries are required to pay inmate workers either the prevailing wage or minimum wage, whichever is higher. Effectively, the state provides the employees which the private company uses to run the business. The inmate is provided with an income which he/she may use in part to support his or her family. In addition, room and board, taxes, and restitution or court costs are deducted from the inmate's wages and five percent is placed in an inmate savings account.[24]

Prison Rehabilitative Industries and Diversified Enterprises

Florida's **Prison Rehabilitative Industries and Diversified Enterprises (PRIDE) Program** is a private non-profit corporation founded in 1981. The PRIDE program is operating in 22 correctional institutions in Florida and involves 38 different industries. The program provides job training and employment opportunities for inmates and helps them to find jobs and to make the transition back to society after their term of incarceration has ended. During 2002, PRIDE trained 3,346 inmates who worked over 3 million hours.[25]

Inmates working in PRIDE industries are paid significantly less than non-inmate workers would receive for the same jobs. However, PRIDE programs do have to absorb certain costs that non-prison industries do not have, including production downtime during lockdowns and daily headcounts, and the costs involved in supervising inmate employees and ensuring the security of the facility.

COMMUNITY SUPERVISION PROGRAMS IN FLORIDA

In Florida, offenders placed on some form of community supervision are supervised by the Florida DOC's **Probation and Parole Field Services**. Probation offices are located in four regions throughout the state, with a regional office supporting the offices in each region. The Central Office of Community Corrections is in Tallahassee. Each of the four regions is divided according to judicial circuits. There are twenty judicial circuits within the four regions and there are several community offices in each circuit, giving offenders easier access for reporting to and meeting with their supervising officers.

Region I, which includes 32 counties, has six judicial circuits and 43 probation offices. As of August 22, 2003, there were a total of 31,699 offenders under supervision. Region II includes 16 counties, five judicial circuits, and 42 probation offices. There were 41,555 offenders under supervision in Region II as of August 22, 2003. Region III comprises four counties and four circuits. There are 31 probation offices in Region III and a total of 40,751 offenders were under supervision as of August 22, 2003. Finally, Region IV, which includes fifteen counties, has five judicial circuits and 53 total probation offices. As of August 22, 2003, there were 39,829 offenders under supervision.[26]

Currently, Probation and Parole Field Services is monitoring and supervising almost 153,000 offenders who are serving all or part of their sentence in the community. Of these, approximately 77 percent are male and 23 percent female. Approximately 62 percent are white, 34 percent black, and 4 percent of other races. Of the offenders under supervision, over 27 percent had committed a violent offense (including murder, manslaughter, sex offenses, robbery, aggravated assault, aggravated battery, or burglary with assault), 35 percent had been convicted of a property crime, and almost 27 percent of a drug offense.[27]

All offenders on community supervision must be monitored by the DOC, including offenders sentenced to community supervision as an alternative to prison as well as those involved in post-release programs. The key element common to nearly all DOC programs is some form of supervision by a correctional probation officer. There are two types of contacts made by probation officers. **Collateral contacts** involve the officer contacting someone other than the offender, such as a spouse, employer, or treatment provider. **Personal contacts** involve the officer contacting the offender directly. This could involve the offender visiting the office of the probation officer or the officer visiting the offender either at home or at the offender's place of employment. The number of contacts required is based on the type of program to which the offender has been assigned and the level of supervision that DOC feels is appropriate.

Pretrial Intervention Programs

Florida has a **Pretrial Intervention Program** (PTI) which allows certain offenders to be diverted from prosecution. The program provides community supervision and treatment for eligible offenders, including first offenders, any offender who has been previously convicted of not more than one nonviolent misdemeanor, and any offender who is charged with a misdemeanor or third degree felony.[28] For an offender to be released to the PTI program, the state attorney, the judge, the program administrator, and the victim must consent. In addition, the defendant must voluntarily agree to the program and must have waived his or her right to a speedy trial. While the offender is in the program, all charges against the offender are continued without final disposition. If the offender does not satisfactorily participate in the program, the pending criminal proceedings may be resumed. However, if the offender successfully completes the PTI program, the court will dismiss the charges and the offender will not be prosecuted. The DOC also has a special PTI program for certain categories of drug offenders which includes substance abuse education and treatment intervention. As of June 30, 2003, there were 7,991 offenders participating in PTI programs.[29]

Probation and Community Control

For the majority of offenders who are supervised by DOC, community supervision is their original sentence. This means that they have been convicted of an offense and sentenced by the court to some form of probation or community control. There are a variety of different programs run by the DOC.

Probation is "a court-ordered term of community supervision under specified conditions for a specific period of time that cannot exceed the maximum sentence for the offense."[30] It involves contacts with probation officers and various other terms and conditions prescribed by law or assigned by the sentencing judge. If the offender violates one or more of the conditions, the court may revoke probation and impose a sentence of incarceration. As of June 30, 2003, there were 106,128 offenders on misdemeanor or felony probation. The state also has several special types of probation. **Administrative probation** is designed for low-risk offenders. If an offender sentenced to regular probation satisfactorily completes half the term, s/he may be placed on "non-contact supervision" for the rest of the term. This means that the offender will not be required to contact the department for the rest of his or her term of supervision. 1,725 offenders were on administrative probation as of June 30, 2003. **Drug offender probation** provides intensive supervision for drug offenders, including individualized treatment plans and probation officers with small caseloads. There were 16,633 offenders in this program as of June 30, 2003. Finally, **sex offender probation** is a community supervision program for offenders who committed specific sex offenses on or after October 1, 1995. Offenders in this program must comply with all conditions of standard probation as well as participate in treatment and counseling, and are required to submit blood samples to the FDLE for registration with the state's DNA data bank.   As of June 30, 2003, there were 2,633 sex offenders in this program.[31]

Community control is a more rigidly structured community-based program for offenders who would otherwise have been sentenced to a period of incarceration. Essentially, the offender is diverted from prison and placed on house arrest, either in his or her own residence or some other non-institutional location. The offender may have some limited freedom authorized by the court (for example, the offender may be allowed to attend school or go to work during certain hours of the day). Offenders are supervised while on community control. In addition, the DOC operates a form of community control for sex offenders, similar to the special sex offender probation program. As of June 30, 2003, there were 12,327 offenders on community control. Of these, 266 were sex offenders.[32]

Offenders placed on probation or community control may be required to comply with a variety of conditions determined by the court. These are outlined in FS §948.03 and may include any of the following:

- the offender must report to a probation officer as directed by the court
- the offender must permit the probation officer to visit him or her at home or at other locations
- the offender must remain employed
- the offender must remain within a specified place
- the offender must make restitution or reparation to the victim
- the offender must support his or her dependents as much as possible
- the offender must not associate with any individuals who are involved in criminal activities
- the offender must submit to random alcohol and/or drug testing
- the offender may not possess, carry, or own a firearm unless the court authorizes it and the probation officer consents
- the offender must attend an HIV/AIDS awareness program
- the offender must complete mandatory public service
- the offender must wear an electronic monitoring device
- the offender must remain confined to a specified residence when not at work or involved in public service activities.

The court decides which of these, if any, will be mandated for the offender.

Some offenders placed on community control may be required to wear an **electronic monitoring** device. These offenders are generally required to remain in their place of residence; effectively they are under "**house arrest**" or "house confinement." They are only allowed to leave their residence to go to work or school, to participate in court-mandated community service activities, or under other specific conditions which are approved by the probation officer. In 1997, the DOC began using the Global Positioning Satellite (GPS) system on offenders who require intensive supervision. It is most commonly used on sex offenders and some other violent offenders. The GPS system allows correctional probation officers to track offenders as they move about within the community. Thus, the officers are able to set "inclusionary boundaries" which define those areas in which the offender must remain as well as "exclusionary boundaries" which define areas into which an offender is not allowed to go (around schools, public playgrounds, the home or office of the victim, etc.). The GPS system consists of a small unit the size of a pager which is worn around the ankle and a larger personal tracking device (approximately the size of a lunchbox) which completes the link to the GPS satellite network and which the offender must carry about with him or her.

If the offender complies with all the terms and conditions of probation or community control, and successfully completes the period of supervision assigned by the court, s/he will be released. According to the DOC, 93 percent of offenders sentenced to community supervision have no new commitments within 24 months after their release from supervision. This includes commitments to prison as well as being recommitted to supervision. Of the rest, one percent are committed to prison and six percent are recommitted to supervision.[33]

Post-Release Supervision

DOC also supervises offenders who have been released from incarceration but are still required to be supervised in the community for some period of time. There are several different types of post-release supervision.

Unlike probation, **parole** is not a sentence. It is actually a form of early release from a sentence of incarceration in which offenders who have not completed their entire terms of incarceration participate in post-release community supervision. In 1983, when the Legislature enacted new sentencing guidelines, the state abolished parole for all offenders whose crimes were committed on or after October 1, 1983. However, inmates sentenced for offenses that were committed prior to that date are still eligible for parole, as are some inmates convicted of capital felonies committed prior to October 1, 1995. No offender sentenced for an offense committed after October 1, 1995 is eligible for parole. As of June 30, 2003, there were 2,197 individuals on parole in Florida. Of these, 743 were Florida cases and 1,454 were cases from other states which have transferred supervision to Florida. There are a total of 5,362 inmates in DOC custody who are eligible for parole.[34]

The **Florida Parole Commission** (FPC) was established in 1941 and remains in existence because there are still inmates in prison who may become eligible for parole in the future. The Commission includes a membership of three individuals who must be residents of the state of Florida. Members are appointed by the state governor and cabinet and confirmed by the state senate. The members are selected from a list of eligible applicants that is provided by the **Parole Qualifications Committee**.[35] This committee includes five members appointed by the governor and cabinet and exists for two years. Its purpose is to advertise for and receive applications for open positions on the FPC, to evaluate those applications, and to present a list of eligible applicants to the governor and cabinet.[36]

According to FS 947.13(1), the FPC has the following duties:

(a) Determining what persons shall be placed on parole...
(b) Fixing the time and conditions of parole...
(c) Determining whether a person has violated parole and taking action with respect to such a violation.
(d) Making such investigations as may be necessary.
(e) Reporting to the Board of Executive Clemency the circumstances, the criminal records, and the social, physical, mental, and psychiatric conditions

and histories of persons under consideration by the board for pardon, commutation of sentence, or remission of fine, penalty, or forfeiture.

(f) Establishing the terms and conditions of persons released on conditional release ... and determining subsequent ineligibility for conditional release due to a violation of the terms or conditions of conditional release and taking action with respect to such a violation.

(g) As the Control Release Authority, determining what persons will be released on control release ... establishing the time and conditions of control release, if any, and determining whether a person has violated the conditions of control release and taking action with respect to such a violation.

(h) Determining what persons will be released on conditional medical release ... establishing the conditions of conditional medical release, and determining whether a person has violated the conditions of conditional medical release and taking action with respect to such a violation.

Conditional release is a program for inmates convicted of and sentenced for violent personal crimes (including murder, manslaughter, robbery, and various sexual offenses) and who either have a prior commitment to state or federal prison or who have been convicted as a sexual predator or habitual offender. When these offenders reach their release dates, they are placed under post-release community supervision for the remainder of their sentence. There were 3,119 offenders on conditional release as of June 30, 2001.[37]

Control release is a program that is used to prevent prison overcrowding by granting early release from prison to selected inmates and placing them under supervision in the community. As of June 30, 2003, there were 143 offenders on control release.[38]

Administrative control release is an alternative to control release. It is similar to administrative probation in that it allows the offender to serve a portion of his or her term of community supervision without having to report to DOC staff. As of June 30, 2003 there were 26 offenders on control release or administrative control release.[39]

There are several other types of post-prison release that are under the control of the DOC. These include provisional release, conditional pardons, county work release, supervised community release, conditional medical release, and addiction recovery supervision. There were 89 offenders on other forms of post-prison release as of June 30, 2003.[40]

BECOMING A CORRECTIONAL OFFICER

The Florida Department of Law Enforcement's **Criminal Justice Standards and Training Commission** (CJSTC) is responsible for setting minimum selection and training standards for correctional officers as well as for law enforcement officers. See Chapter 4 for a more detailed discussion of the FDLE and the CJSTC.

FS §943.13 outlines the minimum standards for employment or appointment as a full-time, part-time, or auxiliary correctional officer in the state of Florida. These standards also apply to individuals employed by a private organization which is under contract to the Department of Corrections. The minimum standards include the following:

- Be at least 19 years old
- Be a United States citizen
- Be a high school graduate or equivalent (G.E.D.)
- Have one's processed fingerprints on file with the employing agency
- Have no felony convictions
- Have no misdemeanor convictions involving perjury or false statements
- Must have received an honorable discharge from the U.S. Armed Forces (if applicable)
- Must pass a physical examination by a licensed physician
- Must pass a background investigation proving good moral character
- Must complete the basic recruit training program (unless exempt under the statute)
- Pass the Florida Officer Certification Examination.

In addition, to become a correctional probation officer, the applicant must have completed a bachelor's degree at an accredited university or college.

The annual salary range for certified correctional officers is $31,547.10 to 47,714.42. There are some salary additives available for certain counties, including Palm Beach, Broward, Miami-Dade, Monroe, Indian River, Martin, Okeechobee, and St. Lucie. Certified correctional probation officers receive salaries ranging from $31,547.10 to $47,714.42 per year, with salary additives for certain counties.[41]

NOTES

1. Florida Department of Corrections, 2002-2003 Annual Report (http://www.dc.state.fl.us/pub/annual/0203/index.html)
2. Florida Corrections Commission home page (http://www.fcc.state.fl.us/fcc/index.html)
3. Florida Department of Corrections, County Detention Facilities - 2002 Annual Report (http://www.dc.state.fl.us/pub/jails/2002/index.html)
4. Miami-Dade County Corrections and Rehabilitation Department website (http://www.co.miami-dade.fl.us/corrections/home.asp)
5. Information obtained from the *2002 Criminal Justice Agency Profile*, available on the Florida Department of Law Enforcement home page (http://www.fdle.state.fl.us/cjst/CJAP/2002/)
6. Miami-Dade County Corrections and Rehabilitation Department website, *op cit*.
7. Broward Sheriff's Office (http://www.sheriff.org/)

8. Broward Sheriff's Office News Release, "BSO Detention Again Earns National Accreditation." January 17, 2002. (http://www.sheriff.org/index.cfm?fuseaction=media.news)
9. Broward Sheriff's Office, *op cit.*
10. *Ibid*
11. Florida Department of Corrections, County Detention Facilities - 2002 Annual Report (http://www.dc.state.fl.us/pub/jails/2002/index.html)
12. Broward Sheriff's Office, *op cit.*
13. Florida Department of Corrections, Florida Corrections: Centuries of Progress (http://www.dc.state.fl.us/oth/timeline/index.html)
14. *Ibid*
15. Florida Department of Corrections home page (http://www.dc.state.fl.us/index.html)
16. *Ibid*
17. Florida Department of Corrections, 2002-2003 Annual Report, *op cit.*
18. *Ibid*
19. Florida Department of Corrections - Frequently Asked Questions Regarding Custody (http://www.dc.state.fl.us/oth/inmates/custody.html#1)
20. Florida Department of Corrections, 2002-2003 Annual Report, *op cit.*
21. Florida Department of Corrections, Florida Corrections: Centuries of Progress, *op cit.*
22. Florida Department of Corrections home page, *op cit.*
23. Florida Department of Corrections - Community Work Squads Earnings and Value Added/Cost Savings Report (http://www.dc.state.fl.us/pub/worksqds/02-03/index.html)
24. Florida Corrections Commission 2000 Annual Report (http://www.fcc.state.fl.us/fcc/reports/final00/Contents.htm)
25. Florida Department of Corrections, 2002-2003 Annual Report, *op cit.*
26. Florida Department of Corrections - Introduction to Information on Florida Adult Community Supervision Offices (http://www.dc.state.fl.us/facilities/comcor/index.html)
27. Florida Department of Corrections, 2002-2003 Annual Report, *op cit.*
28. FS §948.08
29. Florida Department of Corrections, 2002-2003 Annual Report, *op cit.*
30. *Ibid*
31. *Ibid*
32. *Ibid*
33. Florida Department of Corrections - Misconceptions About Community Corrections (http://www.dc.state.fl.us/oth/ccmyths.html)
34. Florida Department of Corrections, 2002-2003 Annual Report, *op cit.*
35. FS §947
36. Florida Parole Commission home page (http://www.state.fl.us/fpc)
37. Florida Department of Corrections, 2002-2003 Annual Report, *op cit.*
38. *Ibid*
39. *Ibid*
40. *Ibid*
41. Florida Department of Corrections - Working for DC (http://www.dc.state.fl.us/employ/index.html)

CHAPTER 9

THE JUVENILE JUSTICE SYSTEM IN FLORIDA

INTRODUCTION

The definition of **juvenile** in Florida is similar to that used in the majority of states in the United States, as well as in the federal system. According to FS §984.03(8),

> "Child" or "juvenile" or "youth" means any unmarried person under the age of 18 who has not been emancipated by order of the court and who has been found or alleged to be dependent, in need of services, or from a family in need of services; or any married or unmarried person who is charged with a violation of law occurring prior to the time that person reached the age of 18 years.

A **delinquent youth** or **juvenile delinquent** refers to any juvenile or youth who has been found by a judge to have committed a delinquent act. A delinquent act is any act that would be a violation of the law if it was committed by an adult.

THE PROBLEM OF JUVENILE CRIME IN FLORIDA

All juveniles under the age of 18 who are charged with a crime are referred to the Florida Department of Juvenile Justice. Between Fiscal Year 1991-92 and Fiscal Year 2000-01, the rate of juvenile delinquency referrals per 1,000 juveniles decreased by 20 percent. During this same period, the number of juveniles in Florida between the ages of 10 and 17 increased by 35 percent. In FY 2000-01, there were a total of 99,770 juveniles arrested for delinquency in Florida. The number of juveniles arrested for felony offenses has decreased 19 percent, from a high of 63,279 in FY 1994-95 to 51,325 in FY 2000-2001. Between FY 1998-99 and FY 2000-01, arrests of juveniles for murder and manslaughter decreased by 30 percent, for armed robbery by 26 percent, for arson by 16 percent, for burglary by 11 percent, and for concealed firearms by 58 percent. Juvenile arrests for drug crimes have also dropped during this period, with a 17 percent decrease in felony marijuana arrests and a 14 percent decline in non-marijuana felony drug cases.[1]

Approximately one-fourth of all juveniles arrested in Florida are girls. During FY 2000-01, there were over 28,500 female juvenile offenders, accounting for over 28 percent of the juveniles arrested for delinquency. Girls have become more heavily involved in violent felony crime. Between FY 1991-92 and FY 2000-01, the number of juvenile females involved in violent felonies almost doubled. However, the trend is beginning to level off at slightly over 3,000 girls arrested for violent felonies each year. Female offenders are significantly more likely than males to have been victims of sexual abuse and to suffer from depression and low self-esteem.[2]

During the 2000-2001 school year, the Florida Department of Education reported 133,530 incidents which were related to school safety. This is a decrease of approximately 26 percent from the number of incidents reported during the previous school year. Every category, including both violent and property crimes, substance use, harassment, fighting, disorderly conduct, and weapons possession showed a decline.[3]

THE FLORIDA DEPARTMENT OF JUVENILE JUSTICE

The **Florida Department of Juvenile Justice** (DJJ) was created in 1994 by the passage of the Juvenile Justice Act. The Department is headed by a Secretary who is appointed by the governor. The Secretary is responsible for the planning and management of all services and programs within the state's juvenile justice system. In 2000, the structure of the DJJ was reorganized around four core functions, each of which is headed by an Assistant Secretary. These four functions are:

- Prevention and Victim Services
- Detention
- Probation and Community Corrections
- Residential and Correctional Facilities

In addition, there is an Administrative Branch responsible for the day-to-day management of the DJJ.

Prevention and Victim Services involves a variety of community- and family-based programs that target at-risk youth. These include after-school programs, non-residential day programs, alternative school programs for juveniles who have been suspended from school, and early intervention programs for students with academic and behavioral problems. In addition, Florida has developed an **Invest in Children** auto tag, a specialty license plate designed to promote community awareness of juvenile delinquency prevention. For each tag sold, twenty dollars goes towards funding services and programs that focus on juvenile delinquency prevention. The tag is generating approximately $500,000 per year for delinquency prevention and intervention programs. A **Bureau of Victim Services** specifically designed for victims of juvenile crime has also been established within the DJJ to help provide victims of juvenile crime with their basic rights.

Juvenile Justice Detention involves placing a juvenile in the care and custody of the DJJ while that juvenile is awaiting adjudication, disposition, or placement in a commitment program. There are two levels of detention in Florida: secure detention and home detention. **Secure detention** involves placing the juvenile in temporary custody within a detention center or facility and is effectively the juvenile justice system equivalent of an adult jail. Juveniles placed in secure detention are considered to be a risk to the public safety and may be held confined for up to 21 days while awaiting judicial disposition (or 30 days in the case of juveniles charged with serious offenses). There are 25 secure juvenile detention facilities in Florida, including one facility that was privatized in January 2003.[4] In **home detention**, the juvenile is released to the custody of a parent or guardian but is under the supervision of the DJJ. The juvenile's movements are restricted and s/he is regularly checked on by Home Detention Officers. Home detention may involve the use of electronic monitoring to restrict the juvenile to his or her home. Home detention is frequently used for juveniles who are awaiting a court date or a placement.

After a juvenile has been charged with a crime, s/he is referred to the DJJ. Each juvenile is assigned to an Intake Officer with the **Probation and Community Corrections** branch. The intake officer is responsible for processing, screening, and assessing the juvenile and for making a recommendation to the court for the disposition of the juvenile. DJJ probation officers based in the Probation and Community Corrections branch are responsible for supervising juveniles who have been given a community-based sentence to ensure that they are complying with all court-ordered conditions.

There are a variety of sanctions that allow the juvenile to remain in the community under the supervision of a DJJ probation officer. **Diversion** programs involve alternatives to formal juvenile justice system processing. These programs are primarily used with first-time offenders who have been charged with minor crimes. Possible sanctions required of juveniles involved in diversion programs may include restitution, community service hours, a curfew, writing a letter of apology to the victim, and counseling. One diversion program, known as **Intensive Delinquency Diversion Services**, provides intensive supervision to juveniles who are at risk of becoming serious chronic offenders. The **civil citation program** allows police to divert minor juvenile offenders out of the juvenile justice system by issuing a civil citation to a juvenile instead of taking him or her into custody. The civil citation requires the juvenile to perform a set number of community service hours, and juveniles who fail to comply with the citation may be referred to the DJJ and may be committed to other programs. The **Teen Court** is a form of community arbitration in which first- and second-time juvenile offenders are tried by a jury of their peers. The court assigns sanctions, such as community service, which must be performed by the juvenile. In addition, juveniles who have completed their assigned sanctions are required to participate in teen court as a jury member. Another diversion program is known as the **Juvenile Alternative Services Program** (JASP). This program takes effect after a juvenile offender has been arrested and an arrest report has been filed. If the DJJ determines that formal judicial processing may not be necessary, the juvenile may be referred to JASP. JASP provides counseling services, conducts home visits, monitors community service hours, and provides referrals to community programs for the juvenile and his or her family members. If the juvenile does not comply with the terms of the program, s/he may be referred back to the DJJ for further action, including formal judicial handling.

Juveniles on **court-ordered juvenile probation** also may be ordered to comply with a variety of court-mandated sanctions and programs. These may include community volunteer hours, restitution, curfew, or attendance at substance abuse counseling or day treatment programs. The juvenile is assigned to a Juvenile Probation Officer who supervises the juvenile to ensure compliance with the conditions of probation. Juveniles who are charged with a serious crime, or who fail to comply with the conditions of probation, may be placed in a DJJ residential facility. After discharge from the facility, the juvenile is placed on **conditional release supervision**, which is similar to adult parole. Juveniles on conditional release supervision are supervised by DJJ officers and may also be required to comply with court-ordered sanctions.

Juvenile Justice Residential and Correctional Facilities are commitment programs for juveniles who have been ordered by the court to serve a period of time in a residential or correctional facility of some type. During FY 2000-01, 8,843 juvenile offenders were committed to residential confinement in Florida.[5] There are a large number of residential facilities located throughout Florida. Almost 90 percent of the available beds are contracted; the remainder are in state-operated facilities.[6]

There are four custody classifications for residential facilities, based on risk to public safety. **Low-risk residential programs** include family group homes and short-term wilderness programs. They are designed for juveniles who require full-time supervision but who are seen as low risk to the public safety. Offenders who have committed a life or first-degree felony, a sex offense, or any offense involving a firearm are ineligible for this level of commitment. Juveniles at this custody level are allowed unsupervised access to the community while spending time in a residential facility. **Moderate-risk residential programs** include intensive vocational work programs, halfway houses, and boot camp programs. The facilities are more secure, either environmentally or physically, and generally have more staff. Most offenders in these programs have committed serious property crimes and are frequent repeat offenders. Juveniles at this custody level are allowed supervised access to the community. **High-risk residential programs** include programs for serious habitual offenders and sex offenders. These juveniles are believed to be of high risk to the public safety and to require close supervision in a more structured setting that is hardware secured (generally using razor wire, security screens, and locks.). Juveniles at this custody level are not allowed access to the community. Finally, **maximum-risk residential programs** provide maximum-security facilities for the most serious, violent, and chronic juvenile offenders. These juveniles are seen as serious risks to the public safety and require full-time custody, care, and supervision in a fully hardware-secure setting. Juveniles at this custody level are also not allowed access to the community. In 2000, Florida opened its first maximum-risk facility for female juvenile offenders, the Florida Institute for Girls. The facility targets girls between the ages of 13 and 18 who have committed serious violent crimes. High-risk and maximum-risk programs are extremely expensive to run: it currently costs almost $46,000 per year for each delinquent girl in the Florida Institute for Girls.[7]

WHAT HAPPENS TO A JUVENILE WHO IS ARRESTED IN FLORIDA

The juvenile justice system differs in several key ways from the adult criminal justice system. After a juvenile is taken into custody by the police, s/he is referred to the DJJ. The juvenile goes through an **intake process** and then may be either released to a responsible adult, such as a parent or guardian, or placed in secure detention while awaiting adjudication or other disposition of his or her case. The DJJ makes a recommendation to the **State Attorney** as to whether the case should be handled through judicial or non-judicial proceedings. There are three options:

- the State Attorney can transfer the case to an adult court

- the State Attorney can divert the case, so that it is handled through a non-judicial proceeding

- the State Attorney can file a petition of delinquency and send the case for judicial proceedings

Under current Florida law, there is no minimum age for transferring a juvenile to an adult court when the charge is punishable by life imprisonment or by death. However, the Florida Statutes do state that no one under the age of 16 may be subject to the death penalty.[8] The decision to transfer a juvenile to an adult court generally depends upon the juvenile's age, the severity of the offense, and the juvenile's arrest history. Florida law requires that any 16- or 17-year old who commits a serious felony with a gun must be tried as an adult and must receive a 10-20-Life sentence to be served in adult prison. The law also requires that any 16- or 17-year old who commits a fourth violent felony be tried as an adult. If a juvenile to be tried as an adult is being held in a juvenile detention center, s/he will be removed and transferred to a section of the local county jail that is reserved for juveniles facing trial in adult court. The juvenile will be tried in the adult criminal felony division of the circuit court and will be treated as an adult in all respects, including possible placement in an adult state prison if s/he is convicted.

Under certain circumstances, a youth may choose to be tried as an adult, rather than to have his or her case handled by the juvenile court. This is an extremely serious decision because a youth who is convicted in an adult court will have an adult criminal record. A youth who is adjudicated delinquent by the juvenile justice system will not have an adult criminal record.

Florida transfers a large number of juveniles to the adult court system each year. However, between FY 1995-96 and FY 2000-01, the number of juveniles transferred to adult court decreased by 61 percent, from 5,350 to 2,817. The decline is attributed to several factors, including an increase in DJJ's residential capacity, the development of maximum-risk DJJ facilities for serious violent juvenile offenders, and other improvements in the juvenile justice system's ability to provide appropriate sanctions and treatment for serious juvenile offenders.[9]

If the case is handled through **non-judicial proceedings**, it may be dismissed or the youth may be diverted out of the system into one of the various available programs, such as teen court or JASP. If the State Attorney files a **petition of delinquency**, an **adjudicatory hearing** is held. This hearing is equivalent to a bench trial in the adult criminal justice system. Youths adjudicated in the juvenile court system do not have the right to a jury trial. At the adjudicatory hearing, the court will determine whether or not the juvenile is delinquent.

If the youth is found not delinquent, s/he will immediately be released from the custody of the juvenile justice system. If the youth is adjudicated delinquent, or if adjudication is withheld, s/he may be held in detention while awaiting **disposition** of the case. During the **disposition hearing**, the court reviews the predisposition report prepared by DJJ, meets with the youth to discuss his or her willingness to comply with any proposed release plan, and gives the victim an opportunity to make a statement commenting on the disposition of the juvenile. Possible dispositions include requiring the juvenile to spend a period of time in a DJJ residential or correctional facility, serving a period of court-ordered juvenile probation, or being assigned to some alternative judicial program, such as community service or work restitution. The most severe penalty that a juvenile offender can receive within the juvenile justice system is commitment to a maximum-risk juvenile correctional facility for a minimum of 18 months and a maximum of three years. The court may also order additional sanctions, such as requiring the juvenile to make restitution to the victim, abide by a curfew, or perform community service. The court may revoke or suspend the juvenile's driver's license, require the juvenile to participate in a substance abuse treatment program, undergo regular drug tests, or attend an educational program. Regardless of the final disposition, when the juvenile completes the disposition program, s/he is released from the custody and supervision of the DJJ.

YOUTHFUL OFFENDERS

Chapter 958 of the Florida Statutes is known as the "**Florida Youthful Offender Act**." FS §958.04(1) discusses the concept of the **youthful offender**, stating that:

> The court may sentence as a youthful offender any person:
> (a) Who is at least 18 years of age or who has been transferred for prosecution to the criminal division of the circuit court...;
> (b) Who is found guilty of or who has tendered, and the court has accepted, a plea of nolo contendere or guilty to a crime which is, under the laws of this state, a felony if such crime was committed before the defendant's 21st birthday; and
> (c) Who has not previously been classified as a youthful offender under the provisions of this act; however, no person who has been found guilty of a capital or life felony may be sentenced as a youthful offender under this act.

Juveniles who have been transferred to adult court may also come under the category of youthful offenders. However, offenders who have been found guilty of a life felony or capital felony are not eligible for youthful offender status.

After conviction in an adult court, a defendant who meets the criteria for classification as a youthful offender is given the opportunity to ask the court for a youthful offender sentence and to present to the court facts to support such a sentence. If the court agrees that a youthful offender sentence is appropriate, the offender may be placed on probation or community control. The court also has the option of withholding adjudication of guilt, which means that the offender will not have a criminal record. The court does have the option of requiring a period of incarceration in a county or community residential facility as a condition of probation. The primary purpose of a youthful offender sentence is to provide a method of control and/or punishment for a young offender who requires close supervision but does not warrant a long-term prison sentence. FS §958.12(1)(a) states that:

> All youthful offenders may be required, as appropriate, to participate in:
> 1. Reception and orientation.
> 2. Evaluation, needs assessment, and classification.
> 3. Educational programs.
> 4. Vocational and job training.
> 5. Life and socialization skills training, including anger/aggression control.
> 6. Prerelease orientation and planning.
> 7. Appropriate transition services.

A youthful offender sentence is an adult sentence, not a juvenile disposition. Youthful offenders are under the jurisdiction of the Florida Department of Corrections (DOC) rather than the DJJ. However, youthful offenders may be placed in a DOC youthful offender facility or a similar minimum security prison rather than a more secure and "hard-core" facility with older adult offenders.

FS §958.11(1) requires the DOC to provide separate institutions and programs for youthful offenders. It also requires that younger offenders be separated from older offenders, stating that:

> Youthful offenders who are at least 14 years of age but who have not yet reached the age of 19 years at the time of reception shall be separated from youthful offenders who are 19 years of age or older, except that if the population of the facilities designated for 14-year-old to 18-year-old youthful offenders exceeds 100 percent of lawful capacity, the department may assign 18-year-old youthful offenders to the 19-24 age group facility.

Youthful offenders may also be sentenced to county-operated boot camp programs if there are specific programs for youthful offenders. FS §958.046 states that youthful offenders and juvenile offenders may not be commingled in boot camp programs.

RECENT LAWS AFFECTING JUVENILES

On May 17, 2000, Governor Bush signed into law what many consider to be the toughest juvenile crime laws in the United States. The purpose of the new **Tough Love** package of juvenile justice reforms is to significantly increase the consequences to serious juvenile offenders and to provide opportunities for rehabilitation to those juveniles who want such help.

One of the most important laws is one that is modeled after the adult **"10-20-Life" law** that was passed in 1999. The new law, which became effective on October 1, 2000, applies to juveniles who are 16 and 17 years old and requires mandatory minimum terms of imprisonment in adult prisons for crimes involving firearms. Prior to the passage of this law, the court had discretion in deciding whether 16- and 17-year-olds who used guns in the commission of crimes should be transferred to adult court for trial. However, the new law requires that these juveniles be tried as adults and given mandatory adult prison sentences. Essentially, if a 16- or 17-year-old who has a prior felony record commits a crime with a gun, s/he must be incarcerated in an adult prison for a minimum of ten years. If the juvenile fires the gun, the mandatory minimum sentence increases to twenty years. If s/he injures or kills someone, there is a mandatory sentence of life in an adult prison. Unlike the adult law, this statute, sometimes known as "**10-20-Life Junior**", does provide judges and prosecutors with some discretion when sentencing first-time offenders. If the juvenile has no prior record of violent felonies or prior gun offenses, did not discharge the weapon, and has no prior commitments to a juvenile residential facility, the court is given sentencing discretion. In addition, prosecutors are given the discretion not to prosecute juveniles under the provisions of this law if they have good reason to believe that there are exceptional circumstances which should prevent prosecution of the juvenile in an adult court.

Another measure included in the Tough Love package is the **four strikes** law. This focuses on habitual juvenile offenders and requires the state to prosecute and punish as an adult any 16- or 17-year-old who is charged with a felony and who has three prior felony convictions.

There are several other Tough Love reforms as well. For example, another bill signed by the Governor increases the length of stay in secure detention for juveniles who have been charged with serious offenses. This provision will allow the courts additional time to process these cases. The bill also authorizes the DJJ to supervise offenders who are placed in post-commitment community supervision for up to one year past the age of 21. In addition, a juvenile who fails to appear in court may be held for up to 72 hours in a secure detention facility prior to his or her next court date. The purpose of this provision is to teach the juvenile to respect the courts and the justice system as a whole.

NOTES

1. *Florida Department of Juvenile Justice 2002 Agency Report*
    (http://www.djj.state.fl.us/agency/Agency%20Report.pdf)
2. Florida Department of Juvenile Justice, Female Juvenile Offenders
    (http://www.djj.state.fl.us/statsnresearch/factsheets/femaleoffenders.html)
3. Florida Department of Education, *Office of Safe Schools-School - Statewide Report on School Safety and Discipline Data, 2000-2001*
    (http://www.firn.edu/doe/besss/sesir/sesir0102.htm)
4. The Southwest Regional Detention Center
5. *Florida Department of Juvenile Justice 2002 Agency Report, op cit.*
6. Florida Department of Juvenile Justice home page (http://www.djj.state.fl.us)
7. *Ibid*
8. Death Penalty Information Center (http://www.deathpenaltyinfo.org/)
9. *Florida Department of Juvenile Justice 2002 Agency Report, op cit.*

CHAPTER 10

DRUGS AND CRIME IN FLORIDA

INTRODUCTION

Drug abuse is a serious problem in Florida. A 1997 survey of Florida residents showed that 76 percent of those polled were concerned about drug trafficking; the only category that produced more concern was that of violent crime (77 percent).[1] The Florida Office of Drug Control estimates that approximately 8 percent of the general population of Florida currently uses illegal drugs, compared to approximately 6.4 percent nationwide.[2] Overall, estimates suggest that there are approximately one million illegal drug users in the state, which is more than 7 percent of all the current drug users in the United States.[3]

The 2003 Florida Youth Substance Abuse Survey, which focused on children in grades six through twelve found that drug use among juveniles is decreasing. Between 2000 and 2003, cigarette use among juveniles has decreased 38 percent, marijuana use decreased by 11 percent, and alcohol use by 10 percent. Abuse of other substances has also decreased.[4] The survey also found that more juveniles perceive drug use as being "wrong" in 2003 than in 2000. Similarly, fewer juveniles view cigarette smoking as "cool." However, the number of juveniles who see the use of alcohol as "cool" increased during this period.[5]

The Florida Department of Law Enforcement reported a total of 126,087 drug arrests in 2002. This included 113,279 adult arrests and 12,808 juvenile arrests. Of those arrested, approximately 90 percent were male and 10 percent female.[6] The number of drug arrests in Florida has decreased from almost 132,000 during the previous year.[7] According to the Florida Department of Corrections (DOC), approximately 29 percent of all offenders admitted to prison in FY 2002-03 had been sentenced for drug crimes, an increase from the FY 1998-99 figure of 27.3 percent. Of these, approximately 87 percent were male and 13 percent female. The majority (65 percent) were black, 33 percent were white, and the remaining 2 percent were of other races. Over 52 percent of drug offender admissions were for the manufacture, sale, and/or purchase of drugs. Of the remainder, approximately 32 percent were admitted for possession, and approximately 16 percent for drug trafficking. As of June 30, 2003, the most common primary offense for which inmates were incarcerated was drugs; approximately 19 percent of all inmates in the Florida prison system were incarcerated for drug offenses.[8] In addition, illegal drug activity may contribute to a considerable portion of personal and property crime in Florida. Offenders who are not arrested for or convicted of drug offenses may still commit crimes that are related to drug abuse. This may include crimes committed while under the influence of an illicit substance or crimes committed to obtain money to obtain drugs. Many offenders are also found to be in possession of a large amount of illegal drugs, indicating that they are dealing in such substances.

In addition to arrests made by Florida law enforcement officers, the Drug Enforcement Agency (DEA) made a total of 3,244 drug arrests in Florida during 2001. The number of DEA drug arrests has been decreasing steadily since 1997, when there were 3,859 arrests.[9]

THE AVAILABILITY OF DRUGS IN FLORIDA

Marijuana

Marijuana is readily available in Florida. Most imported marijuana comes from Jamaica and Mexico, although a considerable amount is also brought down from Canada. Florida is also a major producer of marijuana. Marijuana was found to be grown and cultivated in 54 of the state's 67 counties during 2002. Indoor growing is common as well. Because of the controlled growing environment, marijuana grown indoors is frequently much more potent and thus commands a significantly higher price. The price of outdoor marijuana ranges from $450 to $1,500 per pound, while hydroponically-grown marijuana may sell for $2,500 to $5,000 per pound.[10]

Cocaine

Cocaine appears to be the drug of choice for many users in Florida. The drug, which is grown in Central and South America, is frequently smuggled into the United States through Florida. Florida ports such as Miami have become major entry points for cocaine smuggling, making Florida of significant concern for anti-drug trafficking operations.[11] During FY 2002, powder cocaine sold for between $600 and $1,400 per ounce and $20 to $110 per gram. Powder cocaine is easily converted into **crack cocaine**, which is most commonly available in northern Florida and in the southwestern portions of the state. Crack cocaine sold for between $20,000 and $30,000 per kilogram during FY 2002 and is a major problem in lower socioeconomic areas of the state.[12]

Heroin

Although **heroin** is most common in central and southern Florida, it is easily obtainable in all parts of the state. The most readily available type is South American heroin, but brown powdered heroin and Mexican black tar are also found in the state. During FY 2002, heroin prices ranged from $60,000 to $100,000 per kilogram, $2,200 to $4,000 per ounce, and $60 to $120 per gram. Heroin purity in Florida is extremely high; wholesale heroin (purchased by the kilogram) was generally between 80 and 90 percent pure. Purity levels decreased considerably when the drug was purchased by the ounce or gram.[13]

Methamphetamine

Methamphetamine abuse is becoming a serious problem in Florida, particularly in rural areas, although abuse of the drug in urban and suburban areas appears to be increasing.[14] According to the DEA, the main focal point of methamphetamine distribution in the state is the Tampa Bay area, with much of the state's supply of the drug coming from Mexico and California. Methamphetamine trafficking has also increased in the Jacksonville area. The drug is also increasingly being produced in clandestine laboratories around the state. During FY 2002, the DEA seized 127 clandestine labs and during the first half of FY 2003, 100 labs were seized. This is a significant increase over FY 2001, when only 28 labs were seized throughout the state.[15] During FY 2002, prices for methamphetamine ranged from $70 to $100 per gram and $250 for an "8-ball" (or one-eighth ounce). Purity levels of locally-produced methamphetamine were significantly higher than those of the imported varieties.[16]

Club Drugs

Club drugs include a number of illegal drugs that are found at nightclubs and "rave parties," and on college and university campuses. Common club drugs in Florida include MDMA (Ecstacy) and GHB (gamma hydroxybutyric acid).[17] The main source of MDMA in Florida is Europe. The drug is frequently smuggled into the state on commercial airlines by couriers, as well as being sent through various post and parcel services.[18]

THE FLORIDA OFFICE OF DRUG CONTROL

Because of the serious nature of the drug problem in Florida, Governor Jeb Bush established the **Florida Office of Drug Control** (ODC) in 1999. It is responsible for coordinating all state-wide activities and programs emphasizing the problem of drug abuse and the reduction of that problem. The ODC works in cooperation with federal, state, local, and community agencies and departments. The director of the ODC, James R. McDonough, is known in Florida as the "drug czar," although he does not personally prefer the nickname.

The ODC was created in Chapter 397 of the Florida Statutes. According to FS §379.331(2),

> It is the intent of the Legislature to establish and institutionalize a rational process for long-range planning, information gathering, strategic decision making, and funding for the purpose of limiting substance abuse. The Legislature finds that the creation of a state Office of Drug Control and a Statewide Drug Policy Advisory Council affords the best means of establishing and institutionalizing such a process.

As a result, the ODC has been working, in cooperation with federal, state, local, and community agencies and departments, to develop a state-wide strategy which will focus on solving the drug problem in Florida. The ODC is currently working with a wide variety of agencies, including the Florida Department of Law Enforcement, the Florida Department of Children and Families, the Florida Department of Education, the Florida Department of Juvenile Justice, the Florida Department of Corrections, and a variety of community coalitions, local agencies, and non-governmental organizations, all of whom are committed to stopping the problem of drug abuse.

The result of this collaboration has been the recent implementation of the **Florida Drug Control Strategy**, a long-term concept which incorporates prevention, education, treatment, and law enforcement in a holistic attempt to reduce both the supply of and demand for illegal drugs in the state. The eventual purpose of the program is to reduce drug abuse in Florida by fifty percent. This would mean that less than four percent of Floridians ages twelve and above would use illegal drugs. The Strategy outlines four **strategic goals**:

> GOAL 1: Protect Florida's youth from substance abuse
> GOAL 2: Reduce the demand for drugs in Florida
> GOAL 3: Reduce the supply of drugs in Florida
> GOAL 4: Reduce the human suffering, moral degradation, and social, health, and economic costs of illegal drug use in Florida[19]

The Strategy also has eight specific **performance measures** by which the movement towards these goals may be tracked. The intent is to reach these objectives by the year 2005:

1. Reduce drug abuse in Florida by 2005 to 4% or less.
2. Reduce drug abuse by Florida's youth, ages 1-17) ... to less than 4%.
3. Increase the average age of first-time drug use to 17 years or older...
4. Decrease drug abuse in the workplace by 50%...
5. Reduce the number of chronic drug users in Florida by 50%...
6. Arrest the upward trends of heroin and cocaine-related deaths and bring them down by 50%...
7. Reduce the health costs associated with drug abuse by 25%...
8. Reduce the supply of illegal drugs in Florida by 33%...[20]

One of the most important elements in Florida's Drug Control Strategy is a focus on **prevention**, which is considered by the state to be the key to drug control. The state is implementing a variety of youth prevention programs, focusing on the role of parents in preventing juvenile drug abuse. Programs include sports outreach, the governor's mentoring initiative, specific tobacco and alcohol programs, welfare reform, a focus on minority drug users, and a variety of programs sponsored by the Florida National Guard.

While prevention may be the most cost-effective way to reduce drug abuse, the Strategy also emphasizes **treatment** programs as well. There is also a focus on the need for drug-free workplaces. Florida currently has eight **Drug-Free Workplace Centers**, funded in part by the U.S. Small Business Administration, which assist businesses within the state in the development of workplace policies, prevention training, drug testing, and access to Employee Assistance Programs.

The strategy does not recommend **legalization** of drugs, nor does it encourage a state-supported needle-exchange program for intravenous drug users. While prevention and treatment programs emphasize demand reduction, the **law enforcement** programs outlined in the Strategy focus on reducing the supply of illegal drugs in the state. Recommendations include an emphasis on community policing, a variety of joint operations which involve the cooperation of a variety of police and law enforcement agencies throughout the state, eradication efforts such as crop control, interdiction, and the development of multi-jurisdictional task forces.

FLORIDA DRUG TREATMENT COURTS

In 1989, Florida became the first state in the United States to create a treatment-based **drug court**. The Drug Court Program was first developed in Dade County (now Miami-Dade County) after the state was given a federal mandate to either reduce the inmate population or lose federal funding. After discovering that many inmates had been repeatedly incarcerated on drug charges, the Florida Supreme Court decided to develop a program within the criminal justice system that could deliver treatment services to offenders with drug addictions. This led to the development of the drug court model.[21] As of September, 2003, there were a total of 86 drug courts in Florida, including 38 that have been in operation for over two years, 35 recently-implemented drug courts, and 13 that are still in the planning states.[22]

A drug court is a special court which handles cases involving drug-addicted offenders through the use of extensive supervision and treatment. The court also increases the coordination of various agencies and resources available to drug abusers, increasing the cost-effectiveness of the programs and providing the offender with access to a wide variety of programs and resources.

FS 397.334 discusses the use of treatment-based drug court programs in Florida:

(1) It is the intent of the Legislature to implement treatment-based drug court programs in each judicial circuit in an effort to reduce crime and recidivism, abuse and neglect cases, and family dysfunction by breaking the cycle of addiction which is the most predominant cause of cases entering the justice system. The Legislature recognizes that the integration of judicial supervision, treatment, accountability, and sanctions greatly increases the effectiveness of substance abuse treatment. The Legislature also seeks to ensure that there is a coordinated, integrated, and multidisciplinary response to the substance abuse problem in this state, with special attention given to creating partnerships between the public and private sectors and to the coordinated, supported, and integrated delivery of multiple-system services for substance abusers, including a multiagency team approach to service delivery.

(2) Each judicial circuit shall establish a model of a treatment-based drug court program under which persons in the justice system assessed with a substance abuse problem will be processed in such a manner as to appropriately address the severity of the identified substance abuse problem through treatment plans tailored to the individual needs of the participant. These treatment-based drug court program models may be established in the misdemeanor, felony, family, delinquency, and dependency divisions of the judicial circuits...

Florida drug courts emphasize diversion, probation, and community control. The goal is to divert drug offenders from trial by providing alternatives to traditional criminal justice prosecution for drug-related offenses. Defendants enter the program shortly after arraignment and are given a court-mandated treatment plan which they are required to follow. A sample treatment plan might include:

- submit to urinalysis three times a week

- attend twelve-step meetings three times a week

- attend individual counseling once a week

- attend group counseling once a week

- attend drug court once a month

If a program participant tests negative for drugs and attends the requirement meetings and treatment programs for a prescribed period of time, the treatment plan will be modified by reducing the requirements. Participants are also provided with referrals to various vocational, academic, and health-related programs. Eventually, if participants remain drug-free for a court-specified period of time, the criminal charges against them may be dropped and their records are sealed. If participants do not make adequate progress, the judge may require them to participate in a residential treatment program or send them to jail for a period of time.

The Miami-Dade County Drug Court

The **Miami-Dade County Drug Court** was the first such program in the United States. It involves diversion, supervision, and treatment of drug offenders, focusing on the goal of rehabilitation and providing eligible offenders the opportunity to avoid criminal prosecution. To be eligible for participation, a defendant must be charged with a qualifying drug offense (generally one involving the purchase or possession of illegal drugs) and the State Attorney must agree to the defendant's participation in the program. In general, those defendants who are charged with selling or trafficking in illegal drugs, who have a history of violent crime, or have more than two prior non-drug felony convictions are ineligible for the drug court program.[23]

Participants generally spend between 12 and 18 months in the drug court program, although some may remain in the program for longer periods of time. To participate, defendants must meet all eligibility requirements and must volunteer for drug court. Specific treatment plans are developed for all participants, to meet the individual needs of each individual. The drug court program involves three phases. **Phase I (Detoxification)** takes place in the main treatment clinic in Miami-Dade County and generally lasts between 12 and 15 days (although some individuals require a longer period of time to detoxify). The participant's individual treatment plan is prepared during this phase, and the client participates in both individual and group counseling, 12-step programs, and inpatient treatment. Completion of Phase I requires that the client attend at least 12 scheduled meetings with a primary counselor and have at least seven consecutive clean drug tests.

Phase II (Stabilization) usually lasts from 14 to 16 weeks, but can be as short as two months or as long as one year or more. During this phase of the program, participants continue to participate in counseling sessions and 12-step meetings, and are required to submit to regular urine tests. **Phase III (Aftercare)** may last for eight months or more and involves helping the participant prepare for a drug-free future. Clients participate in educational and vocational programs, attend job development classes, and are given assistance in finding employment.

Clients who successfully complete the drug court program are released from drug court supervision and are not prosecuted for the drug charges. Clients who fail to comply with the requirements of the program are subject to sanctions by the drug court judge. Consistent and repeated violations may result in removal from the drug court program and prosecution in criminal court on the original charges.[24]

The Broward County Drug Court

Broward County's Drug Court program has been in operation since 1991. It is the third oldest drug court program in the country, and one of the largest. The focus of the Broward Drug Court is treatment of the offender's drug addiction and the underlying causes of that addiction. It is a diversion program, serving as an alternative to a prison sentence. The goals of the program are:

> To intervene with criminal offenders who are charged with the purchase or possession of a controlled substance and other substance abuse related charges, and to offer a one year positive alternative to incarceration. To break the cycle of addiction and criminal justice involvement, a variety of individualized treatment services are utilized to restore the individual as a productive member of society. Treatment goals include abstinence, improved life management skills, improved interpersonal relationships, and involvement in community support groups.[25]

The Broward Drug Court accepts adults (18 years or older) who have no prior felony convictions and who are charged with a second or third degree substance abuse felony (generally felony drug possession). Currently, offenders who commit non-drug offenses while under the influence of drugs or to support a drug habit are not eligible for the program. Offenders who are accepted into the drug court program go through an out-patient treatment program that may involve:

- weekly or daily counseling, therapy, and education contacts with the Broward County Alcohol and Drug Abuse Services Division

- urinalysis checks

- bi-weekly status hearings before the drug court judge

151

- participation in a rehabilitation program that involves educational, vocational, family, medical, and other services

Offenders who violate the court's prohibition against drug use may be sanctioned in a variety of ways, including:

- required daily court appearances
- electronic monitoring
- residential treatment
- incarceration

The Broward Drug Court is a diversion program. The defendant waives his or her right to a speedy trial and enters a plea of not guilty. S/he then enters the pre-trial drug court program and participates for a minimum of one year. If the defendant successfully completes all the program requirements, the drug-related charges against the defendant are dismissed. The program reports a recidivism rate of less than four percent for program graduates.[26]

NOTES

1. Chiricos, Ted, *Fear of Crime and Related Perceptions in Florida-1997* (Tallahassee, Florida: Florida State University, School of Criminology and Criminal Justice, June 1998).
2. Florida Office of Drug Control (1995). *Florida Drug Control Strategy, 1999-2005* (http://www.myflorida.com/myflorida/government/governorinitiatives/drugcontrol/strategy.html)
3. *Ibid*
4. Florida Office of Drug Control (2003). *2003 Florida Youth Substance Abuse Survey.* (http://www.myflorida.com/cf_web/myflorida2/healthhuman/substanceabusementalhealth/publications/fysas/special4.html)
5. *Ibid*
6. Florida Department of Law Enforcement, *Statewide Arrests by Age and Sex, 2002* (http://www.fdle.state.fl.us/FSAC/Crime_Trends/total_Index/FL_arrests-age-sex.asp)
7. Florida Department of Law Enforcement, *Statewide Arrests by Age and Sex, 2001* (http://www.fdle.state.fl.us/FSAC/UCR/2001/CIFA_annual01.pdf)
8. Florida Department of Corrections, 2002-2003 Annual Report (http://www.dc.state.fl.us/pub/annual/0203/index.html)
9. Office of National Drug Control Policy (2003). *State of Florida: Profile of Drug Indicators.* (http://www.whitehousedrugpolicy.gov/statelocal/fl/fl.pdf)
10. *Ibid*
11. DEA Fact Sheet: *Florida* (http://www.usdoj.gov/dea/pubs/states/florida.html)
12. Office of National Drug Control Policy (2003). *State of Florida: Profile of Drug Indicators, op cit.*
13. *Ibid*

14. *Ibid*
15. DEA Fact Sheet: *Florida, op cit.*
16. Office of National Drug Control Policy (2003). *State of Florida: Profile of Drug Indicators, op cit.*
17. *Ibid*
18. DEA Fact Sheet: *Florida, op cit.*
19. Florida Office of Drug Control (1995). *Florida Drug Control Strategy, 1999-2005, op cit.*, p.3-2
20. *Ibid*, p.3-4
21. Florida State Courts, Drug Court Program (http://www.flcourts.org/index.html)
22. Office of National Drug Control Policy (2003). *State of Florida: Profile of Drug Indicators, op cit.*
23. Miami-Dade County Drug Court (http://www.jud11.flcourts.org/programs_and_services/drug_court.htm)
24. *Ibid*
25. Broward County Drug Court (http://www.browarddefender.com/drugct.htm)
26. *Ibid*

APPENDIX

WEB SITES OF INTEREST

There is a wealth of information on Florida and the Florida criminal justice system available on the world wide web. Below are a selection of web sites that may be of interest to students.

GENERAL FLORIDA WEB SITES AND LEGAL INFORMATION

http://www.myflorida.com/
> The official web site of the State of Florida. This site provides a variety of information services for citizens and for state and local government.

http://www.leg.state.fl.us/
> This site is the official home page of the Florida State Legislature. It includes links to both the Senate and the House of Representatives. This page also includes links to the Florida Constitution and the Florida Statutes. You can search the statutes by keyword for the specific subject of interest.

http://myfloridalegal.com/
> This is the web site of Florida Attorney General Charlie Crist.

INFORMATION ON POLICE IN FLORIDA

http://www.fhp.state.fl.us/
> The web site of the Florida Highway Patrol.

http://www.fdle.state.fl.us/
> The web site of the Florida Department of Law Enforcement.

http://www.mdpd.com/
> The web site for the Miami-Dade Police Department.

http://www.sheriff.org/
> The home page for the Broward County Sheriff's Office.

http://police.dadeschools.net/
> The Miami-Dade Schools Police Department web site.

http://ci.ftlaud.fl.us/police/
> The web site for the Fort Lauderdale Police Department.

http://www.cityoforlando.net/police/
> The web site for the City of Orlando Police Department.

http://www.fpca.com/stagencies.htm
> The web site for the Florida Police Chiefs Association. This site includes links to most police departments and law enforcement agencies in the state.

INFORMATION ON THE COURTS IN FLORIDA

http://www.flcourts.org/
> The web site of the Florida State Courts. This site includes links to many Florida courts throughout the state.

http://www.flabar.org/
> The web site for the Florida Bar.

http://www.floridabarexam.org/
> This is the web site for the Florida Board of Bar Examiners.

INFORMATION ON CORRECTIONS IN FLORIDA

http://www.dc.state.fl.us/
> The web site for the Florida Department of Corrections.

http://www.fcc.state.fl.us/
> The web site for the Florida Corrections Commission.

http://www.co.miami-dade.fl.us/corrections/home.asp
> This is the web site for the Miami-Dade County Corrections and Rehabilitation Department.

http://www.state.fl.us/fpc/index.shtml
> The web site for the Florida Parole Commission.

INFORMATION ON THE FLORIDA JUVENILE JUSTICE SYSTEM

http://www.djj.state.fl.us/
> The web site of the Florida Department of Juvenile Justice

http://www.fldoe.org/
>The web site of the Florida Department of Education

http://www.state.fl.us/cf_web/
>The home page of the Florida Department of Children and Families

INFORMATION ON DRUGS IN FLORIDA

http://www.whitehousedrugpolicy.gov/statelocal/fl/fl.pdf
>The Office of National Drug Control Policy provides a large amount of information on drug use statistics and drug prevention efforts in Florida.

http://www.usdoj.gov/dea/pubs/states/florida.html
>A DEA fact sheet on drugs in Florida.

http://www.myflorida.com/myflorida/government/governorinitiatives/drugcontrol/
>The web site of the Florida Office of Drug Control.

http://www.fadaa.org/
>This is the web site of the Florida Alcohol and Drug Abuse Association.